Freehand Sketching

For Engineering Design

Freehand Sketching
For Engineering Design

Jon M. Duff
William A. Ross
Purdue University

PWS Publishing Company

I(T)P **An International Thomson Publishing Company**

Boston • Albany • Bonn • Cincinnati • Detroit • London • Madrid • Melbourne • Mexico City • New York • Paris • San Francisco • Singapore • Tokyo • Toronto • Washington

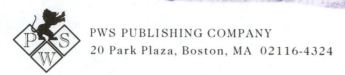

PWS PUBLISHING COMPANY

20 Park Plaza, Boston, MA 02116-4324

Copyright © 1995 by PWS Publishing Company, a division of International Thomson Publishing Inc.

I(T)P™ International Thomson Publishing
The trademark ITP is used under license.

For more information, contact:

PWS Publishing Co.
20 Park Plaza
Boston, MA 02116

Nelson Canada
1120 Birchmount Road
Scarborough, Ontario
Canada MIK 5G4

International Thomson Publishing Asia
221 Henderson Road
#05-10 Henderson Building
Singapore 0315

International Thomson Publishing Europe
Berkshire House 168-173
High Holborn
London WCIV 7AA
England

International Thomson Editores
Campos Eliseos 385, Piso 7
Col. Polanco
11560 Mexico D.F., Mexico

International Thomson Publishing Japan
Hirakawacho Kyowa Building, 31
Chiyoda-ku, Tokyo 102
Japan

Thomas Nelson Australia
102 Dodds Street
South Melbourne, 3205
Victoria, Australia

International Thomson Publishing GmbH
Königswinterer Strasse 418
53227 Bonn, Germany

Library of Congress Cataloging-in-Publication Data

Duff, Jon M.
    Freehand sketching for engineering design / Jon M. Duff, William A. Ross.
        p.   cm.
    ISBN 0-534-93966-X
    1. Freehand technical sketching.   2. Three-dimensional display systems.
    I. Ross, William A.   II. Title.
    T359.D84   1994
    620'.0042'0285 — dc20   94-37330
                                                                       CIP

Sponsoring Editor: Jonathan Plant
Developmental Editor: Mary Thomas
Production Editor: Monique A. Calello
Editorial Assistant: Lai Wong
Manufacturing Coordinator: Ellen Glisker
Marketing Manager: Nathan Wilbur

Interior Design: The West Highland Press
Cover Art: Jon M. Duff Technical Art
Cover Design: Monique A. Calello
Cover Printer: Henry N. Sawyer Co., Inc.
Text Printer: Courier/ Kendalville

Printed and bound in the United States of America.
94 95 96 97 98 99 — 10 9 8 7 6 5 4 3 2 1

Contents

Preface

This text–workbook of engineering graphics problems contains homesheet and lab exercises for engineering and technology students. It is based on the concept that modern graphics may be started freehand and subsequently formalized by using CAD tools. It includes a concise overview of basic CAD modeling techniques and a full complement of engineering drawing and modeling exercises. They cover model visualization through orthographic multiviews, missing view problems, isometric pictorials, auxiliary views, sectional views, assemblies, and dimensioning basics. Each chapter contains a brief overview of the topic followed by numerous sketching problems intended to serve as pre-CAD visualization exercises.

Sketching Exercises in Support of CAD Modeling

This text makes an ideal lab manual for use in combination with *Modeling For Design Using AutoCAD* and *Modeling for Design Using SilverScreen*, both by Stewart, Bolluyt, and Oladipupo. Because the generic nature of the problems in this book, it may also be used in conjunction with any 2D or 3D CAD software textbook. Although the emphasis in the text is on 3D modeling and object visualization, the inclusion of traditional engineering drawing practices such as orthographic, missing view, auxiliary, and sectional views make it highly useful with 2D CAD courses as well.

How to Use This Workbook

Two philosophical decisions by the authors heavily influenced the structure of this text and accepting them is important to you, the user of this text-workbook.

- Modeling is an introduction to sketching because the student should view sketching as a modeling exercises — albeit limited by pencil and paper.

- Isometric sketching is presented before orthographic reading because pictorial sketches are a major tool for visualizing missing views.

The book is organized around an introductory chapter that explains the terminology and standard techniques used in 3D model building in CAD software. All subsequent chapters then use these model-building techniques and apply them to the standard practices and conventions used in engineering design graphics and technical drawing. The book is written so the reader will be able visualize, sketch, and solve the modeling geometry either prior to or during a work session with 3D CAD software. The intent of the book is to strengthen the relationship between visualization, preliminary pencil sketching, and the modeling–drawing methods commonly found in 3D CAD software. In order to reinforce the value and appearance of planning with sketches for computer-aided design, all illustrations, figures, examples, and exercises in the book are presented in a sketched format.

The typical arrangement of material in each chapter includes

- a brief overview and introduction to the chapter topic;

- practical examples from business or industry showing how the topic is related to CAD; and

- sketching exercises based on the chapter topic. Because this is a supplemental text or lab manual, the bulk of each chapter is devoted to practical exercises progressing in difficulty from easy or moderate to complex.

Acknowledgments

We wish to thank the many individuals who contributed to the success of this text-workbook. Jonathan Plant of PWS Publishing Company recognized the importance of sketching in the education of engineers and technologists. Without his support and encouragement we would not have been able to complete this project. Thanks to Monique Calello for riding herd on the authors, keeping them at least within reason, on schedule. A sincere appreciation goes to those graphics teachers who took the time to review the manuscript. We would have liked to incorporate all of their suggestions but production and time constraints limited implementing many of their fine ideas. They certainly are on file for the next edition. Special thanks go to Dr. Ted Conway from the University of Akron, Dr. Larry Genalo of Iowa State University, Dr. Steve Howell at Northern Arizona University, Dr. Dennis Lieu at The University of California-Berkley, Professor Menardi at Tufts University, Dr. Paul Morrison who teaches at the British Columbia Institute of Technology, Dr. Stephen Reed from Weber State University, Dr. Thomas Singer at Sinclair Community College, and Dr. Kelly Waldal at the University of Regina for their careful reviews. Any mistakes in the printed version are not theirs, but solely the authors' responsibility. And finally, a special thanks goes to the students at Purdue University who were patient with us while we took them, often kicking and screaming, from the drawing board to sketching for CAD.

Jon M. Duff
William A. Ross

Introduction

To Teachers

To assist the student, all exercises are placed on grids, scaled, and include a computer world and user coordinate system icon. Once the student has visualized and sketched a solution, the completed sketches can be directly used to construct accurate three-dimensional (3D) models on all major CAD software programs, principally, AutoCAD, CADKEY, and SilverScreen. Throughout this book, 3D Cartesian coordinate systems and user–defined construction planes are shown in conjunction with grids or dimensions for all sketching exercises. The purpose of identifying X, Y, Z coordinate systems and construction planes on sketching exercises is to enable students to construct 3D computer models directly from their sketched solutions. Because of its widespread use and for consistency, the graphical representation of coordinate systems and gridded reference planes shown on all exercises is based on the familiar user coordinate system (UCS) icon utilized in AutoCAD software. The UCS icon, familiar to AutoCAD users for many years, is graphically incorporated in all sketching exercises as depicted in the following examples.

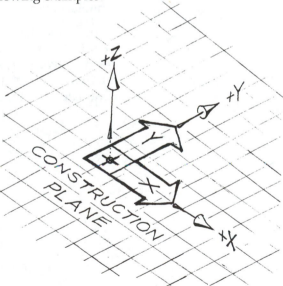

UCS Icon and its associated user-defined and movable construction plane.

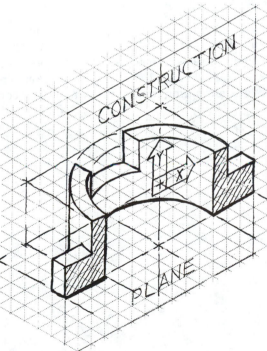

Applied Example: UCS icon showing the orientation of a vertically positioned construction plane.

We are sure that you will want to use a standard CAD text along with this sketching text-workbook. Some of you may be perplexed as to why 3D modeling was presented first. This decision is based on a paradigm that acknowledges that engineering design, whether in a designer's mind or put in tangible form, is a 3D exercise. You may be forced to represent the 3D concept on a two-dimensional surface — either in a sketch, drawing, or CAD model. But the thinking must be 3D to begin with. This is what we try to instill in each and every student. All sketches then are representative of this 3D mental model. The sooner you start thinking three-dimensional thoughts, the more powerful the design process. Because we believe that sketching is the vehicle for planning CAD, such sketching should lead in the most natural sense to CAD modeling.

To Students

The vast majority of you were good sketchers in kindergarten and first grade. You sketched because it was the most efficient way for you to explain your world. After all the years, you are back to the same point. Sketching is almost tool-independent. You can do it anywhere, with almost any material. Sketching is immediate. It involves little investment in time or ego. Spend a few hours on a detailed drawing and your natural inclination is to avoid changing it, even in the face of overwhelming evidence that your design simply doesn't work.

Sketching allows you to be efficient and productive in CAD. Sitting down at a CAD workstation with little conception as to how you are going to solve a problem is the surest way to guarantee that you will be inefficient. Because sketching doesn't have a fixed tool box, you might entertain a solution that were you to do all of your thinking with the computer you might overlook.

How good of a sketcher do you have to be to be a successful designer? Your sketches must firstly communicate to yourself. Many landmark designs began life as seemingly unintelligible squiggles. But at some time you must communicate your ideas to coworkers, your boss, or a board of directors. At that time, a sketch must communicate its technical and geometric data exactly. This is the level of sketching to which you should aspire.

Most of the chapter examples and all of the workbook pages are done in sketch form. The text on these pages is for the most part hand-lettered. This was done intentionally to guide your development. If you conscientiously use these as good examples, you should reawaken the sketcher in yourself. You'll be ready to use sketching to plan and evaluate your engineering designs, preparing them for eventual CAD completion.

1 3D Modeling

The Importance of Sketching

The importance of freehand technical sketching for the purpose of graphically conceiving and communicating preliminary design ideas cannot be overemphasized. The process of sketching promotes spatial thinking, visualization, and logical, systematic ways of creating geometry. Computer-aided design tools, particularly 3D modeling software, may then be efficiently used to construct the engineering geometry for design, analysis, manufacturing, and documentation.

Although technical sketching may appear artistic, it is not considered artistic drawing. It should be thought of as a convenient method for quickly expressing and communicating ideas graphically. Freehand technical sketching is highly portable in that it requires only pencil and paper. Although any type of paper may be used for sketching, square and isometric grid papers are very popular because the grid lines make sketching and measurement easier. Figure 1-1 shows typical use of square and isometric grid paper for technical sketches. Throughout this book, problems are presented on square and isometric grid paper.

Fig. 1-1. Sketching on square and isometric grids.

Sketching Technique

Technical sketching is done freehand and rapidly; not with a straight edge and drawing instruments. Sketches should be made with dark, clearly visible lines that may be easily interpreted. For purposes of this text, we will assume that all sketches will be made with either a wooden or a mechanical graphite pencil, not with ink.

When sketching, rest the pencil on the second finger and hold it by the thumb and index finger as shown in Fig. 1-2. In order to avoid tension or fatigue, allow the forearm to rest on the table or drawing surface while the wrist and fingers are used to sketch. When

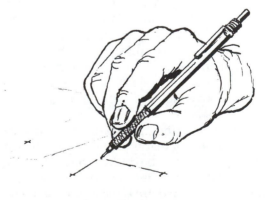

Fig. 1-2. Hand position for technical sketching.

creating a sketch, do not tape the paper down. Instead, leave it free so that it can be turned to a convenient angle for sketching.

Straight lines are normally sketched by first marking the endpoints of the line. This provides a starting point and an end point for each line to be sketched. Horizontal lines, as shown for right-handed people in Fig. 1-3(a), are typically sketched from left to right with an easy motion of the wrist and fingers pivoted about the muscle of the forearm. Left-handed people normally sketch horizontal lines from right to left. Vertical lines, as shown in Fig. 1-3(b), are best sketched with a downward, pulling motion. As you sketch each line, it is a good idea to keep your eye on the end point of the line.

To sketch curved lines for arcs, cylinders, and rounded shapes, first, draw lines to indicate the center of the curve. Next, insert points along the path of the curve as shown in Fig. 1-4. For a cylindrical shape, between 4 and 8 points are recommended. Now, complete the curved arc with a light construction arc and check to see that the curve is properly proportioned. Finally, darken the curve with a bold, dark line.

Model Building — General Conditions

Computer-aided design (CAD) is used to generate views for engineering drawings by one of two methods. Views may either be "electronically drafted" or constructed in 2D-CAD, as shown in Fig. 1-5(a), or projected and "extracted" from revolved three-dimensional models in 3D CAD as shown in Fig. 1-5(b).

2D CAD: Producing two-dimensional orthographic multiview drawings with 2D CAD has many similarities to sketching and manual drafting. Views are created and aligned using 2D geometric construction methods such as template or construction lines, tangency, polygons, trimming and extending of lines, automatic line types, and a variety of other tools. Construction of isometric and auxiliary views in 2D CAD also relies on similar 2D construction methods such as boxing-out, grid construction, and normal projection from lines representing the edge views of inclined surfaces.

3D CAD: Producing orthographic multiview drawings using 3D CAD is more a matter of moving the viewer or rotating the object so that the desired view is obtained as shown in Fig. 1-5(b). Standard views of the model, such as front, top, or right sided are typically aligned with the 3D axis system of the CAD program. Since any view is possible with a three-dimensional model, isometric

Fig. 1-3(a). Sketching horizontal lines.

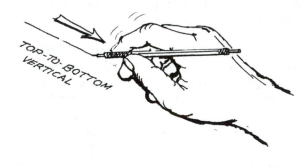

Fig. 1-3(b). Sketching vertical lines.

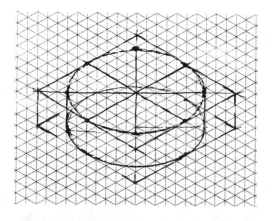

Fig. 1-4. Laying out points to sketch a curve.

pictorial and auxiliary views require revolving the model or the user's line of sight into the correct viewing position. In auxiliary views this is accomplished by aligning the viewer's line of sight at a right angle or normal to a particular inclined or oblique feature on the model by means of a movable construction plane with its own local coordinate axis system. If actual flat two-dimensional views are required, the 3D CAD program must also have the capability to convert or smash the three-dimensional model into a true two-dimensional format on any user-defined construction plane containing a desired view as shown in Fig. 1-6. The resulting 2D view may then be used for drafting and documentation purposes.

Although faster and more accurate than manual drawing methods, 2D CAD has the same limitation as the drawing board. It is two-dimensional. As a tool for visualizing and creating objects that may be viewed from their front, top, right side, auxiliary, or isometric positions, 3D CAD offers much more power than 2D CAD. Therefore, the focus of this chapter and the premise of this book are on methods of using 3D CAD to visualize, model, and generate required views for engineering drawings directly from 3D models.

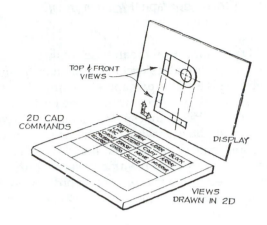

Fig. 1-5(a). Views constructed in 2D CAD

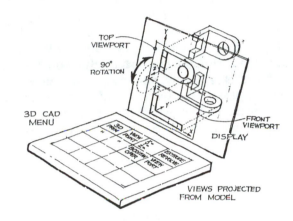

Fig. 1-5(b). Views projected from a 3D CAD model.

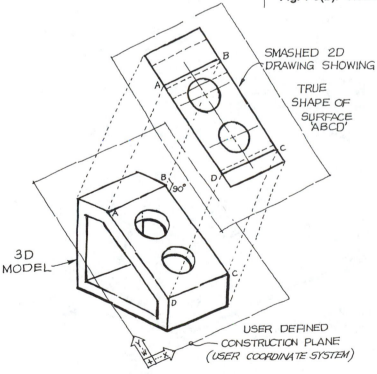

Fig. 1-6. Smashing 2D images from 3D CAD models.

Movable Construction Planes in 3D

All 3D CAD programs provide the user with a virtual "3D space" in which to construct models. In order to use this modeling space accurately and efficiently, the user must have some method of controlling the position and size of every 3D object in that space. Hence, 3D CAD programs furnish the user with a predefined and fixed Cartesian coordinate system containing X, Y, and Z axes for referencing the absolute position of each vertex, edge, surface, and object in the model. This coordinate system is commonly referred to as the *world coordinate system*.

In the real world, measurements are seldom made from a single reference point that is absolute or fixed. Instead, measurements are taken relatively or locally from any convenient point to any other point. For example, if the corner of a room is considered to be the origin of the world coordinate system (0, 0, 0), how would you measure the width of a table inside the room? Using the world coordinate system, you must locate each corner of the table relative to the world coordinate system, i.e. (4, 6, 3) for the first table corner and (5, 9, 3) for the opposite diagonal. So how wide is the table? A rather

awkward way of measuring don't you think? To solve this problem in 3D CAD, a movable local coordinate system called the *user coordinate system* (UCS) is supplied to the user. Figure 1-7 illustrates this concept. The local UCS can be repositioned on-the-fly by the user, similar to a tape measure, and placed anywhere and at any orientation within the modeling space.

One of the most powerful ways of using a movable user coordinate system is to use it as a reference or construction plane. A *construction plane* (also referred to as a work plane or a reference plane) can be thought of as an infinitely large 2D drawing plane that can be positioned anywhere in 3D space. Since most people feel comfortable drawing in 2D, the construction plane can be used as a drawing surface as well as a plane on which to position 3D objects. Unlike 2D CAD, the construction plane may be moved freely to any other location in 3D space. In popular CAD programs such as AutoCAD, the construction plane , or user coordinate system, is visually indicated by the UCS icon, showing the orientation of the local X, Y, and Z axes. Figure 1-7 illustrates the concept of the construction plane shown with the UCS icon.

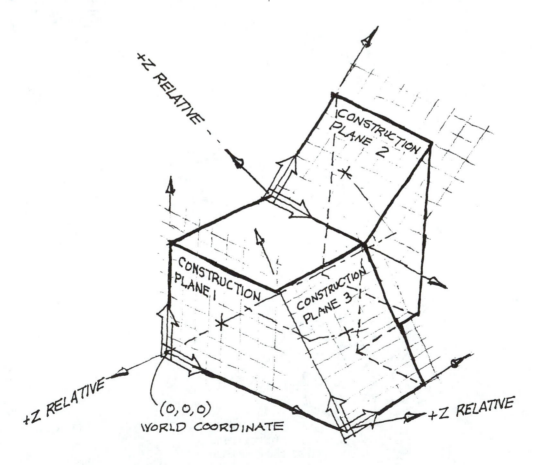

Fig. 1-7. Movable coordinate systems and construction planes.

Modeling Primitives

Perhaps the most common method of three-dimensional modeling is by combining 3D geometric *primitives*. Most 3D CAD programs come with a standard set of primitives, which include, but are not limited to, the box, cylinder, cone, and sphere. The primitives may then be selectively combined to build the various external features of an object as shown in Fig. 1-8. Primitives are typically specified by the user according to their overall dimensions, such as diameter and height for a cylinder. When primitives are input by the user, they are typically attached to or positioned with respect to the current location of the construction plane.

There are currently three distinctively different methods used for geometric modeling in 3D CAD programs; wireframe, surface, and solid models. Of these three methods, solid primitives give the most complete and unambiguous description of an object. In other words, a hole through a block will be treated as a true hole in a solid block and not as a circular opening in a hollow box. Because the primary focus of this text is on sketching and describing 'real world' objects made of solid materials such as metal, plastic, or wood, all objects in this chapter and throughout the book are referred to and treated as solid objects.

In 3D CAD, not all objects have sharp well defined edges that can be easily shown with lines. To describe the boundaries of surfaces on curved primitives such as cylinders, cones, and spheres, special lines are required. These display lines, often referred to as *tessellation lines*, useful in visually clarifying the description of complex curved boundaries.

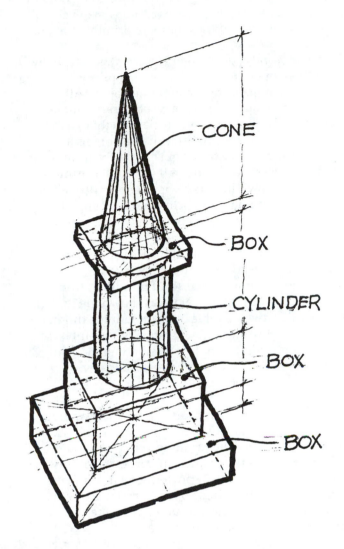

Fig. 1-8. Building with 3D primitives.

Boolean Operations

As described previously, a primary method of model building is by stacking a series of 3D primitive building blocks to "additively" construct a model. Although useful as a starting point for solid modeling in 3D CAD, this method is limited unless the user can define a range of relationships between overlapping or connected primitives. These relationships are called Boolean operations named after English mathematician George Boole (1815–1864), who developed a mathematical system in which all variables are assigned a value of either 1 or 0. *Boolean operations* allow the user to perform three types of operations: union, difference, and intersection. In all Boolean operations, the area of interest is where the common volumes of the 3D primitives intersect or overlap. It is at the zone of overlap or intersection where the Boolean operation takes place. Although typically performed on only two primitives at a time, Boolean operations may be performed on a set of three or more primitives at once.

The *union operation*, shown in Fig. 1-9(a) is essentially an additive operation with all selected primitives being merged into a new single composite object. All overlapping volumes of the new object are counted only once. The new object may be thought of as a single "higher order" primitive that maintains a recoverable subset of the original primitives. In other words, the user may "undo" a higher order primitive and break it down into its composite primitives if need be. This continuing or branching relationship of operations is referred to as Boolean tree.

The *difference operation* is a subtractive operation that creates a composite solid by subtracting the overlapping volume of one set of primitives from another set of primitives. Note, as shown in Fig. 1-9(b), that there are two possible outcomes for the difference operation. The difference operation is a useful technique for doing simple but important modeling operations such as creating holes in solids by subtracting cylinders from larger solids.

The *intersection operation* takes only the overlapping 3D volume common to all selected primitives and makes that common space the resulting object. Although less intuitive than the union and difference operations, the intersection operation is a powerful method of creating complex objects in a single operation. Figure 1-9(c) shows the finished object resulting from the intersection of two solid primitives.

Extruded and Revolved Objects

Solid objects with thin walls and complex symmetrical exterior shapes cannot always be modeled easily with geometric primitives and Boolean operations. Many objects, because of their shape, can be easily created as extruded and revolved objects by sweeping their profiles along or around an axis. Just as you can mentally decompose a complex solid object into regular primitives and Boolean operations, you can imagine the cross section through a solid object and create an accurate profile of this cross section. The profile can then be used in one of two ways to create a solid object.

Extruded solid objects are typically made by sweeping a closed profile shape along an axis. Normally, the

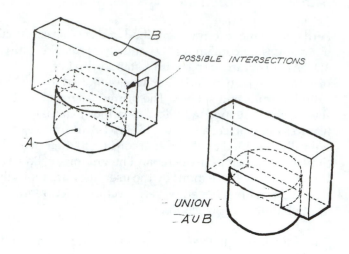

Fig. 1-9(a). The union operation.

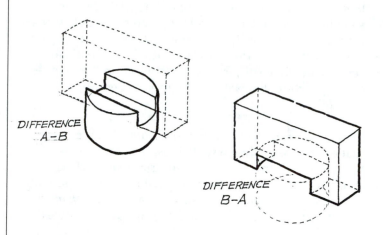

Fig. 1-9(b). The difference operation.

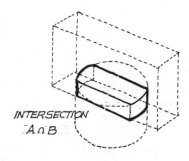

Fig. 1-9(c). The intersection operation.

profile is perpendicular to the axis of extrusion as shown in Fig. 1-10(a).

Revolved solid objects are made by *sweeping* or revolving a profile shape around an axis. Although solids of revolution are usually swept through a 360° rotation, any convenient angle between 0° and 360° may be used as shown in Fig. 1-10(b).

Modeling by Sketching Exercises

The sketching exercises on pages 9 through 19 are designed to provide sketching practice in the basic model building techniques commonly used in 3D CAD and solid modeling. The modeling logic involved in these exercises is intended to serve as a useful starting point for visualizing, sketching, and modeling the problems that follow in this text.

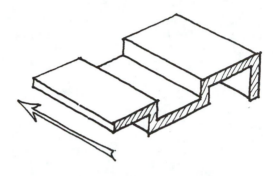

Fig. 1-10(a). Example of extruded shape.

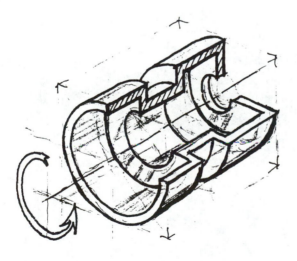

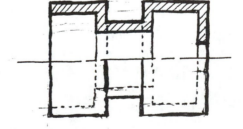

Fig. 1-10(b). Example of revolved shape.

GIVEN THE SIZE DESCRIPTIONS BELOW, MAKE AN ISOMETRIC SKETCH OF EACH PRIMITIVE BASED ON THE ORIENTATION OF THE USER COORDINATE SYSTEM (UCS). NOTE THE + AND − DIRECTION OF THE Z AXIS. DARKEN IN ONLY VISIBLE EDGES.

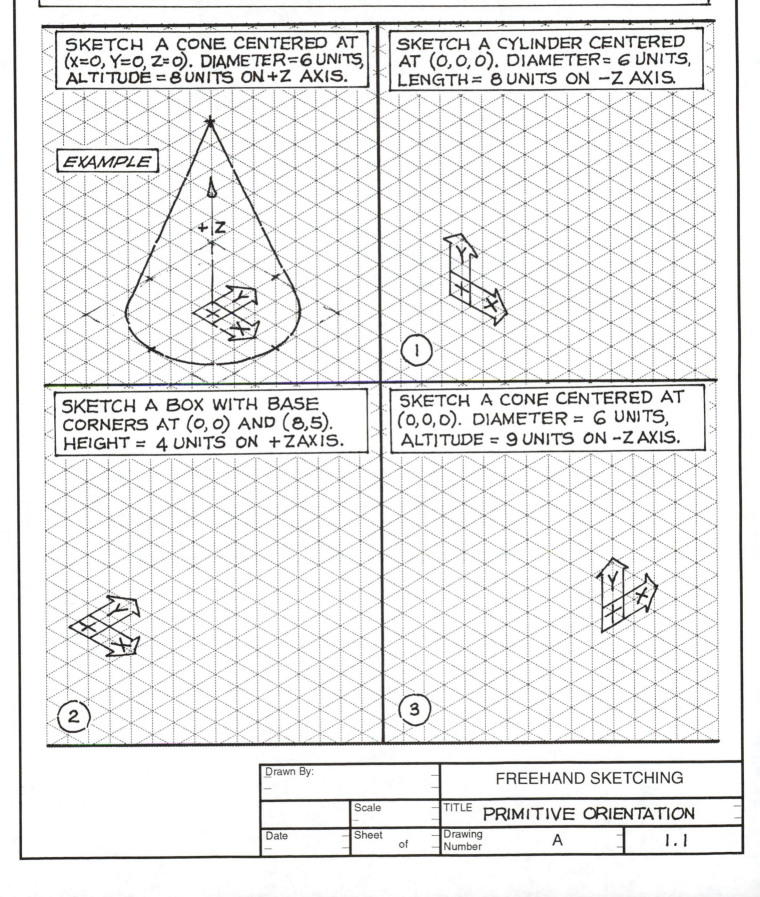

SKETCH A CONE CENTERED AT (x=0, y=0, z=0). DIAMETER=6 UNITS, ALTITUDE = 8 UNITS ON +Z AXIS.

EXAMPLE

SKETCH A CYLINDER CENTERED AT (0, 0, 0). DIAMETER= 6 UNITS, LENGTH = 8 UNITS ON −Z AXIS.

①

SKETCH A BOX WITH BASE CORNERS AT (0, 0) AND (8,5). HEIGHT = 4 UNITS ON +Z AXIS.

②

SKETCH A CONE CENTERED AT (0, 0, 0). DIAMETER = 6 UNITS, ALTITUDE = 9 UNITS ON −Z AXIS.

③

Drawn By:		FREEHAND SKETCHING		
	Scale	TITLE PRIMITIVE ORIENTATION		
Date	Sheet of	Drawing Number	A	1.1

GIVEN THE TOP & FRONT VIEWS OF THE CITY PRIMITIVES, MAKE A PICTORIAL SKETCH OF THE SCENE ON A SEPARATE SHEET OF ISOMETRIC GRID PAPER. DARKEN IN ONLY VISIBLE EDGES. OPTIONAL: SHADE IN ALL SURFACES FACING TO THE RIGHT.

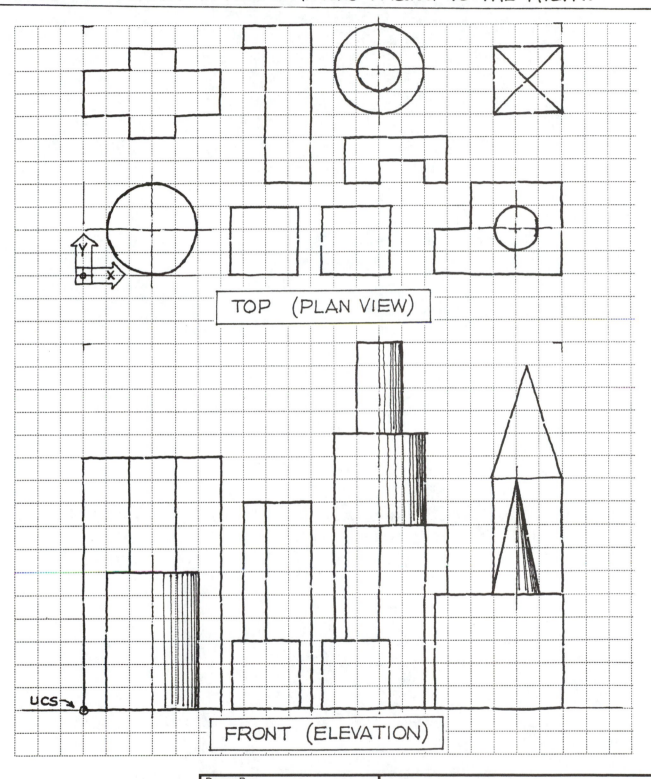

TOP (PLAN VIEW)

FRONT (ELEVATION)

UCS

Drawn By:		FREEHAND SKETCHING		
	Scale	TITLE PRIMITIVE VISIBILITY		
Date	Sheet of	Drawing Number	A	1.2

BASED ON THE OVERLAPPING SOLID PRIMITIVES SHOWN BELOW, AND
THE BOOLEAN OPERATIONS ASSIGNED, DARKEN IN ALL VISIBLE EDGES
OF THE RESULTING COMPOSITE SOLID AS SHOWN IN THE EXAMPLES.

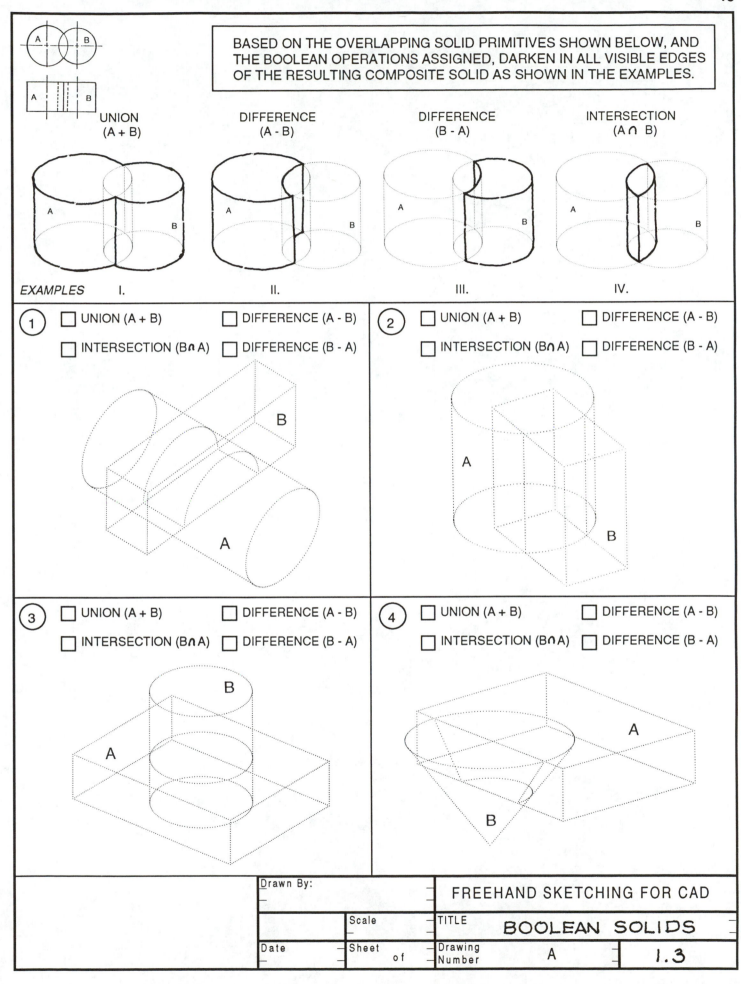

UNION
(A + B)

DIFFERENCE
(A - B)

DIFFERENCE
(B - A)

INTERSECTION
(A ∩ B)

EXAMPLES   I.   II.   III.   IV.

1 ☐ UNION (A + B)   ☐ DIFFERENCE (A - B)
   ☐ INTERSECTION (B∩A)   ☐ DIFFERENCE (B - A)

2 ☐ UNION (A + B)   ☐ DIFFERENCE (A - B)
   ☐ INTERSECTION (B∩A)   ☐ DIFFERENCE (B - A)

3 ☐ UNION (A + B)   ☐ DIFFERENCE (A - B)
   ☐ INTERSECTION (B∩A)   ☐ DIFFERENCE (B - A)

4 ☐ UNION (A + B)   ☐ DIFFERENCE (A - B)
   ☐ INTERSECTION (B∩A)   ☐ DIFFERENCE (B - A)

Drawn By:		FREEHAND SKETCHING FOR CAD	
	Scale	TITLE BOOLEAN SOLIDS	
Date	Sheet of	Drawing Number A	1.3

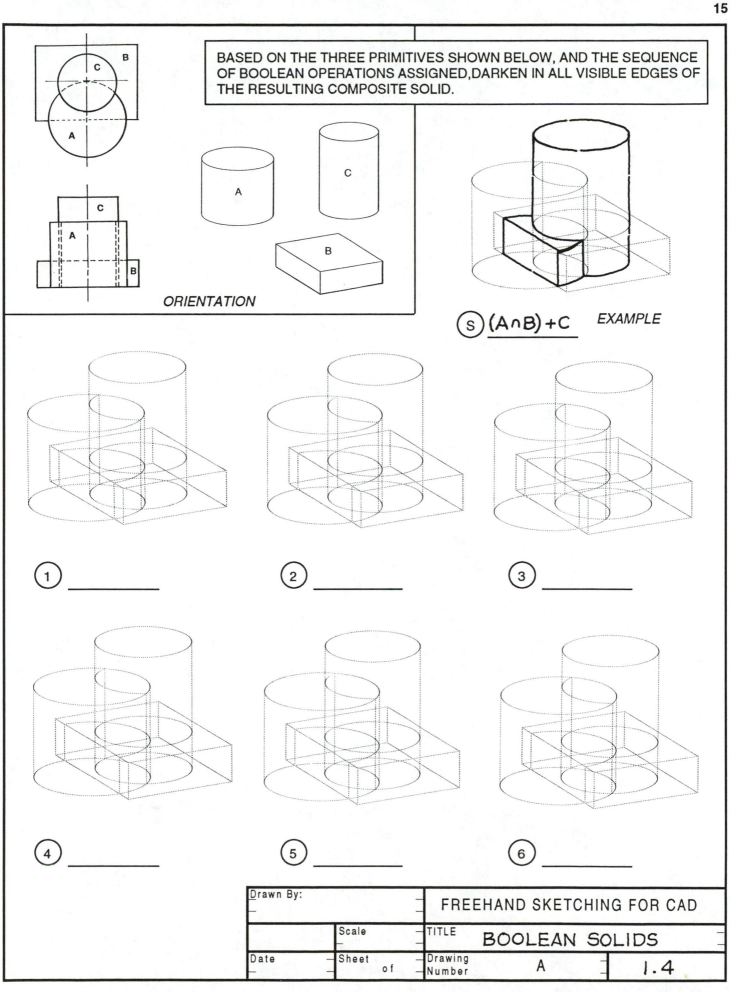

BASED ON THE THREE PRIMITIVES SHOWN BELOW, AND THE SEQUENCE OF BOOLEAN OPERATIONS ASSIGNED, DARKEN IN ALL VISIBLE EDGES OF THE RESULTING COMPOSITE SOLID.

ORIENTATION

(S) (A∩B)+C   *EXAMPLE*

1 _____

2 _____

3 _____

4 _____

5 _____

6 _____

Drawn By:		FREEHAND SKETCHING FOR CAD	
	Scale	TITLE BOOLEAN SOLIDS	
Date	Sheet of	Drawing Number A	1.4

17

EXTRUDE THE PROFILES AS SHOWN. USING THE LOGIC OF
BOOLEAN INTERSECTION, DARKEN IN THE VISIBLE EDGES OF
THE RESULTING SOLID MODEL.

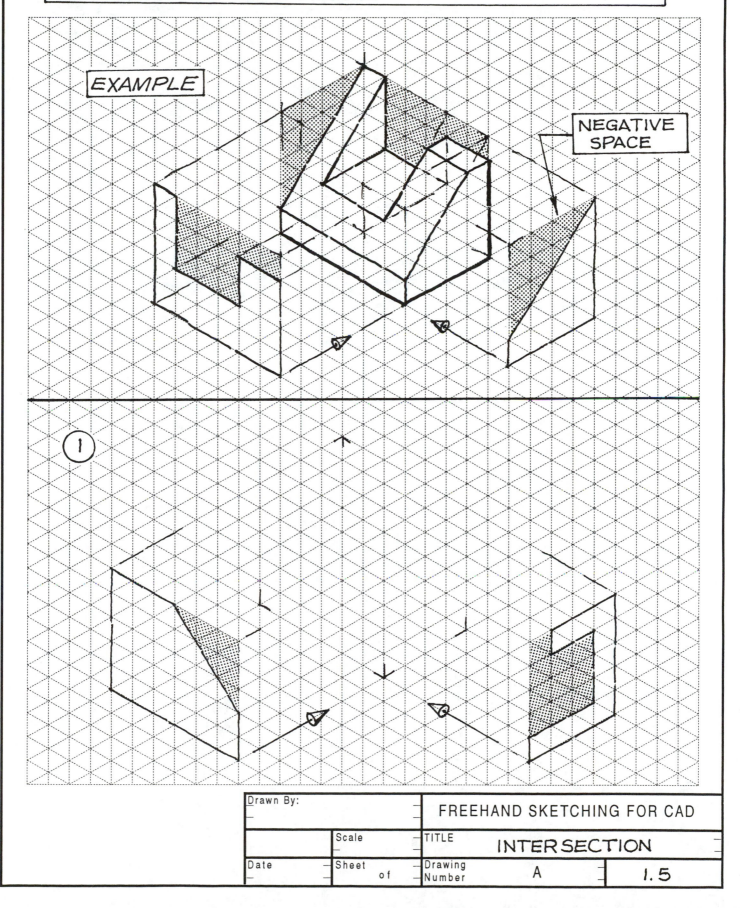

EXAMPLE

NEGATIVE SPACE

1

Drawn By:		FREEHAND SKETCHING FOR CAD	
	Scale	TITLE INTERSECTION	
Date	Sheet of	Drawing Number A	1.5

EXTRUDE THE PROFILES AS SHOWN. USING THE LOGIC OF
BOOLEAN INTERSECTION, DARKEN IN THE VISIBLE EDGES OF
THE RESULTING SOLID MODEL.

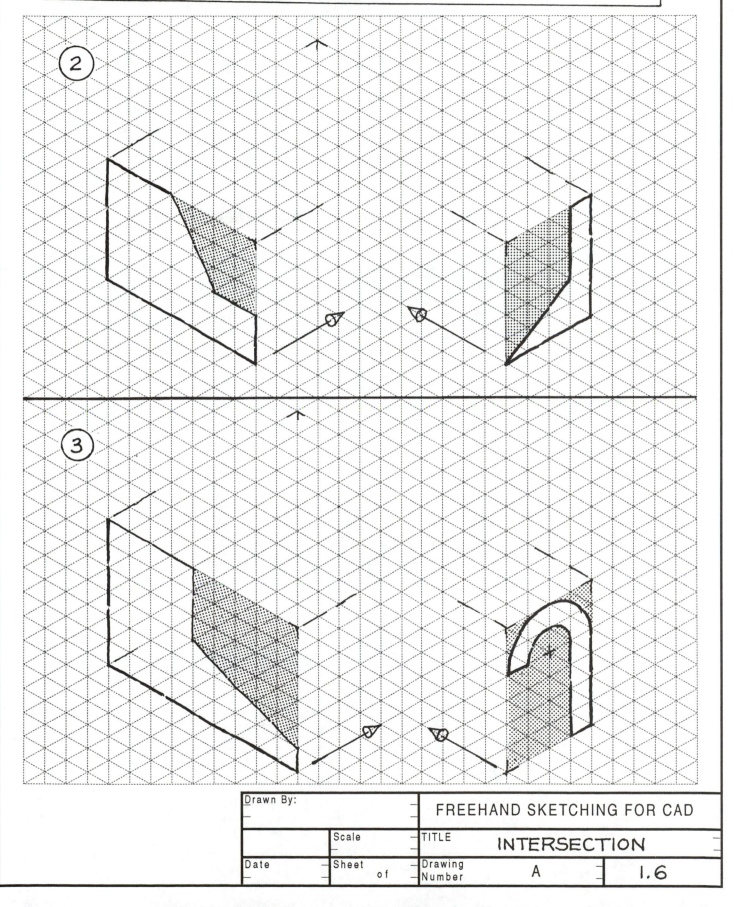

Drawn By:		FREEHAND SKETCHING FOR CAD		
	Scale	TITLE	INTERSECTION	
Date	Sheet of	Drawing Number	A	1.6

2 Orthographic Sketching

Orthographic Views — General Conditions

An *orthographic view* (ortho meaning at right angles) presents two of the three dimensions of height, width, and depth in one view. When these three dimensions are known, the object is unambiguous. The view can be made by different people at different locations within acceptable variation. Two or more views drawn at the same scale are usually arranged so that the two share a common dimension. That allows the views to be *read*, that is, the geometry to be understood. When views are arranged in this manner they are said to be *aligned*. See Fig. 2-1. In practice, large industrial drawings may be on separate sheets, making reading difficult.

Orthographic views show no perspective. Conditions that are parallel in space are shown parallel on the drawing. The perspective in Fig. 2-1 is for comparison only and is not an aligned view.

The *front view* is usually the view that shows the characteristic shape of the object or the position in which the object is usually found. Additional views are positioned as needed above (top view), to the right or left (side views), or below (bottom view). Thin objects such as shims, gaskets, or plates require only one view and a note as to their thickness (Fig. 2-2). Cylindrical objects may require only two views. The more complicated the object, the more views are needed to fully describe object geometry.

Sheet 2.0 on page 25 shows both pictorial and orthographic views of the same object. The *pictorial* is used for visualization. The orthographic views are used to establish the exact relationship of geometric features such as planes, holes, and the like. Viewing directions have been established in the pictorial view that corresponds to orthographic views. Study each viewing direction and its resulting orthographic view.

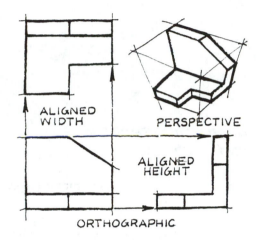

Fig. 2-1. Aligned views.

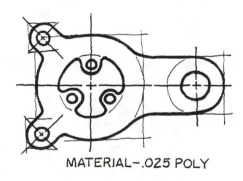

Fig. 2-2. A One-view orthographic sketch.

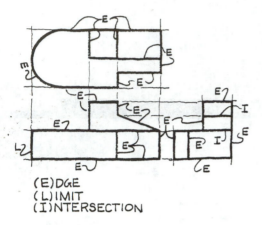

(E)DGE
(L)IMIT
(I)NTERSECTION

Fig. 2-3. Solid lines on a drawing.

Representation of Intersections, Surfaces, and Limits

In the orthographic views, lines are used for very specific purposes.

Solid Lines. A visible plane edge, intersection, or limit (Fig. 2-3).

Dashed Lines. An edge, intersection or limit obscured by material between it and the observer (Fig 2-4).

Lines of Symmetry. Non geometric lines used to show the center of a hole or a cylinder (Fig. 2-5).

Assignment: On the orthographic views of Sheet 2.0, identify each of the lines by type (solid, dashed, symmetry), and by geometric feature (edge, limit, intersection). Practice your technical lettering on each label.

Practical Example

In Fig. 2-6 a pictorial sketch of an electrical part has been prepared. This is often the first step in designing a part — producing a pictorial sketch. In the next chapter you will gain more experience in pictorial sketching.

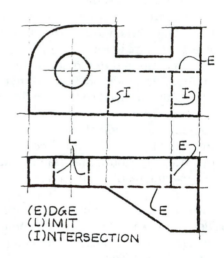

(E)DGE
(L)IMIT
(I)NTERSECTION

Fig. 2-4. Dashed lines.

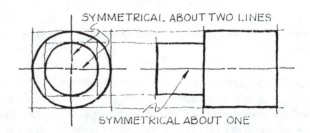

SYMMETRICAL ABOUT TWO LINES

SYMMETRICAL ABOUT ONE

Fig. 2-5. Lines of symmetry.

Note that you can visualize a part's general shape quite easily from a pictorial sketch. From the pictorial traditional orthographic views can be prepared. Follow these steps to prepare orthographic views (Fig 2-7):

1. Decide which views are necessary and sufficient.

2. Rough out the overall dimensions of the views. Keep them aligned.

3. Add the detail and work *between the views*. That is, you may have to simultaneously work on two views, adding from one to the other until they are complete.

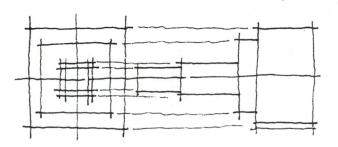

Step1 Layout Overall Dimensions

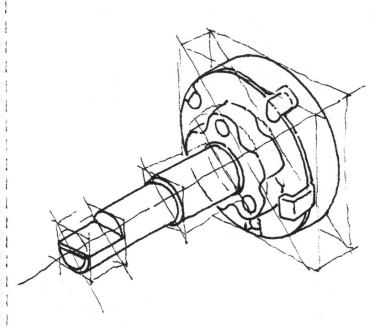

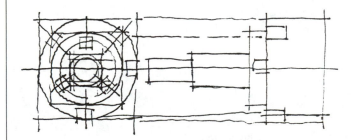

Step 2 Rough Out Details

Fig. 2-6. Pictorial sketch.

CAD Example

A designer will work from pictorial or orthographic sketches in order to produce a CAD drawing. The overall strategy is much the same—define the overall geometry first and then add the detail.

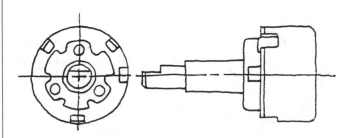

Step 3 Add Detail

Fig. 2-7. Steps in completing orthographic views.

Figure 2-8 shows the same electrical part in its rough
layout, (a), edited layout, (b), and detailed layout, (c).
Note that to simplify construction, the UCS is relocated
as necessary.

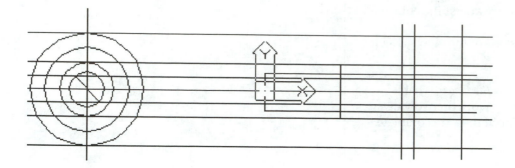

Fig. 2-8(a). Rough layout in CAD.

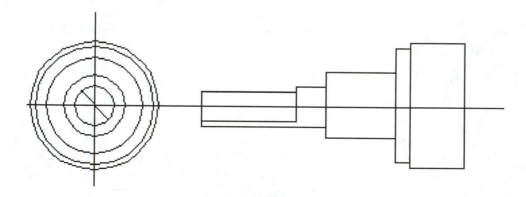

Fig. 2-8(b). Edited layout in CAD.

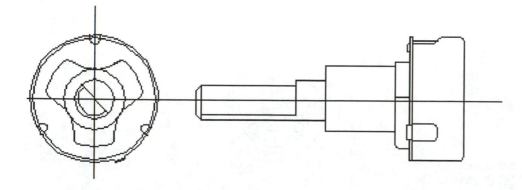

Fig. 2-8(c). Detailed layout in CAD.

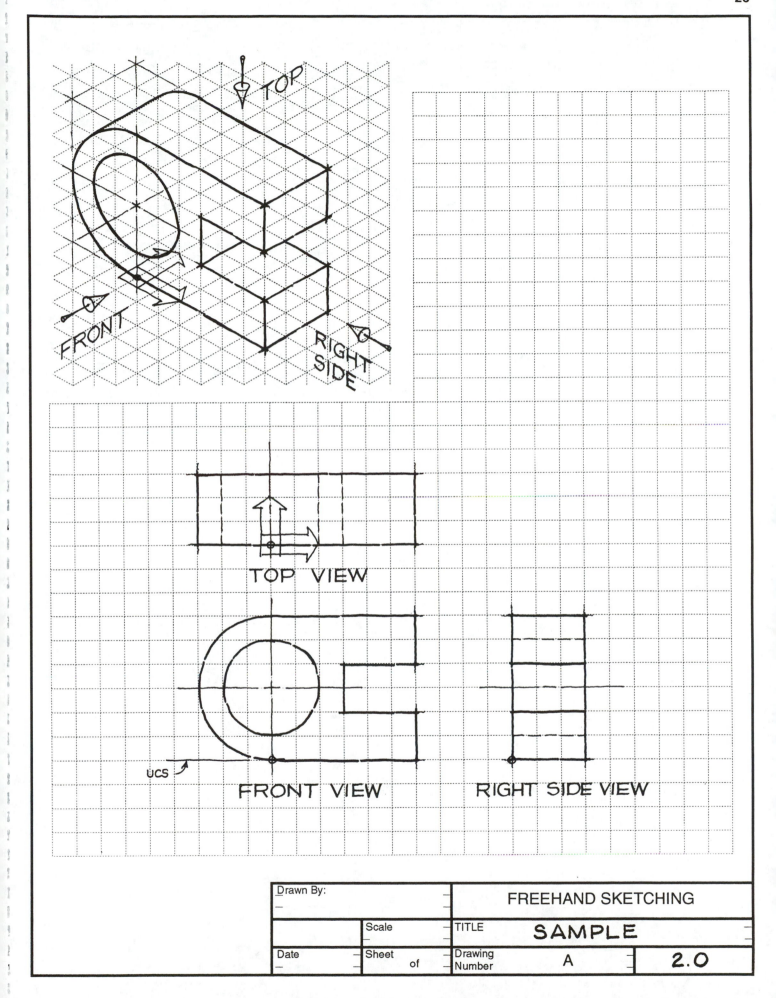

TOP

FRONT

RIGHT SIDE

TOP VIEW

UCS

FRONT VIEW

RIGHT SIDE VIEW

Drawn By:		FREEHAND SKETCHING		
	Scale	TITLE	SAMPLE	
Date	Sheet of	Drawing Number	A	2.0

27

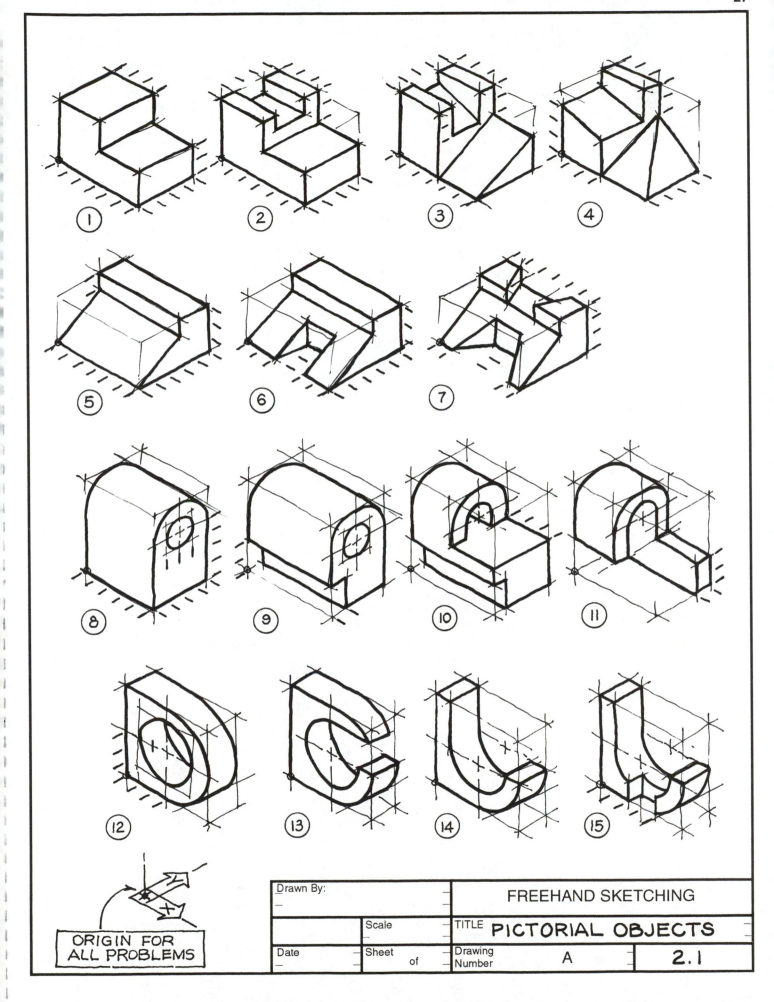

ORIGIN FOR
ALL PROBLEMS

Drawn By:		FREEHAND SKETCHING		
	Scale	TITLE **PICTORIAL OBJECTS**		
Date	Sheet of	Drawing Number	A	**2.1**

29

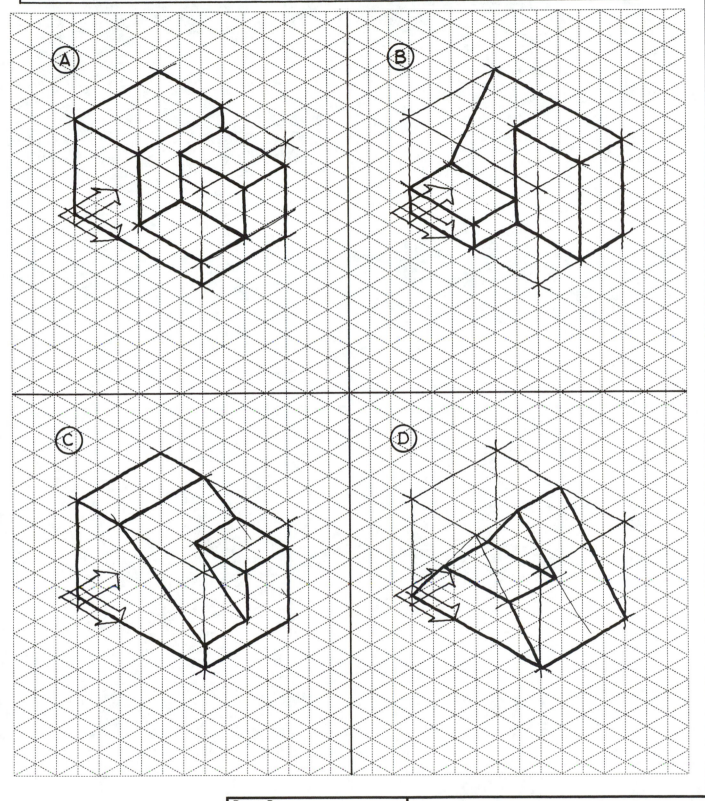

COMPLETE THREE-VIEW ORTHOGRAPHIC SKETCHES OF THE FOLLOWING OBJECTS. USE ORTHO GRID PAPER.

Drawn By:		FREEHAND SKETCHING	
	Scale	TITLE PICTORIAL OBJECTS	
Date	Sheet of	Drawing Number A	2.2

31

COMPLETE THREE-VIEW ORTHOGRAPHIC SKETCHES OF THE
FOLLOWING OBJECTS.   USE ORTHO GRID PAPER.

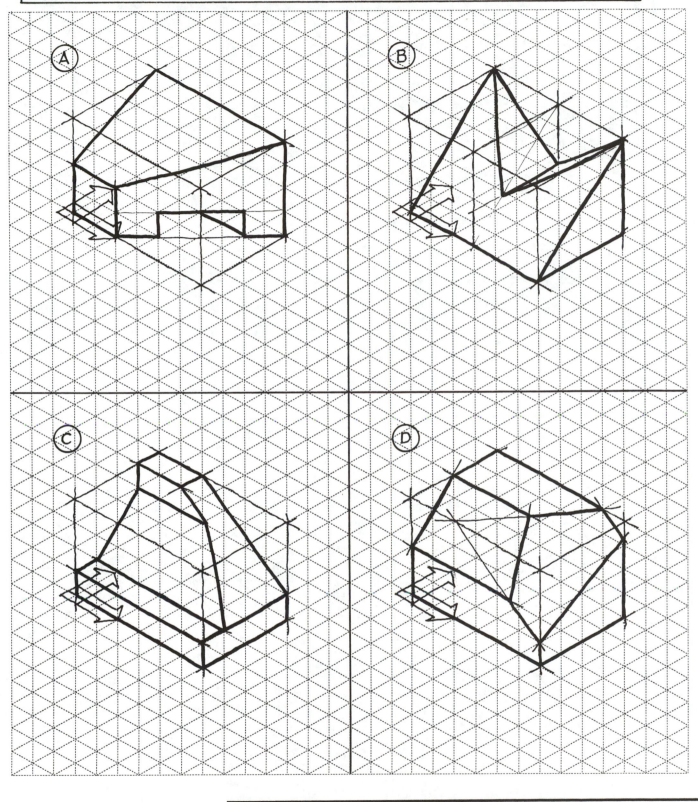

Drawn By:		FREEHAND SKETCHING	
	Scale	TITLE PICTORIAL OBJECTS	
Date	Sheet of	Drawing Number A	2.3

COMPLETE THREE-VIEW ORTHOGRAPHIC SKETCHES OF THE
FOLLOWING OBJECTS. USE ORTHO GRID PAPER.

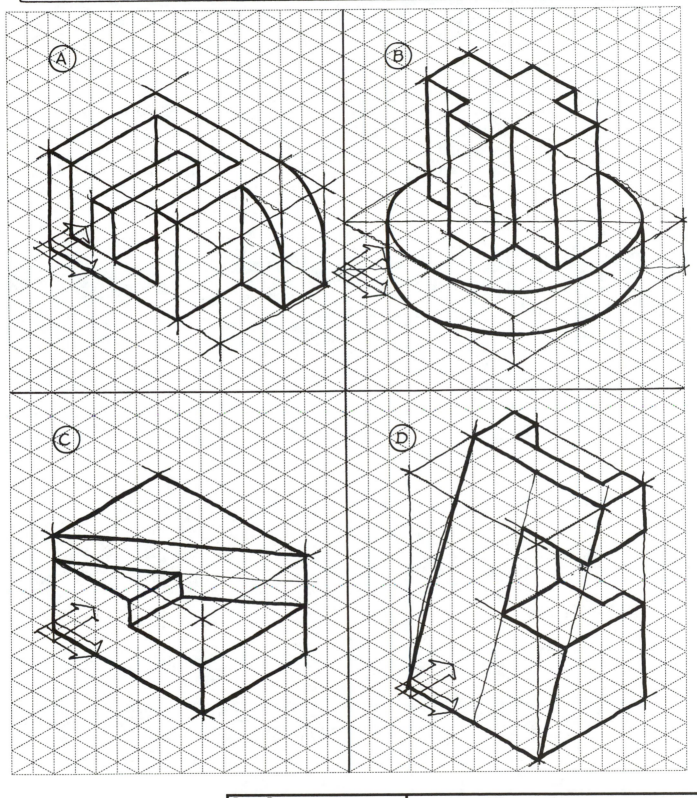

Drawn By:		FREEHAND SKETCHING		
	Scale	TITLE PICTORIAL OBJECTS		
Date	Sheet of	Drawing Number	A	2.4

COMPLETE THREE-VIEW ORTHOGRAPHIC SKETCHES OF THE FOLLOWING OBJECTS. USE ORTHO GRID PAPER.

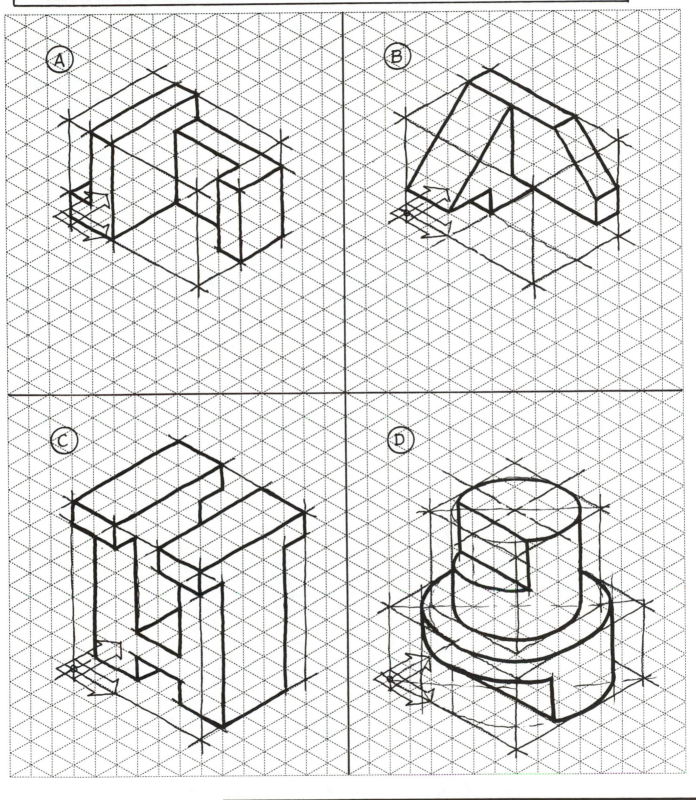

Drawn By:		FREEHAND SKETCHING	
	Scale	TITLE PICTORIAL OBJECTS	
Date	Sheet of	Drawing Number A	2.5

37

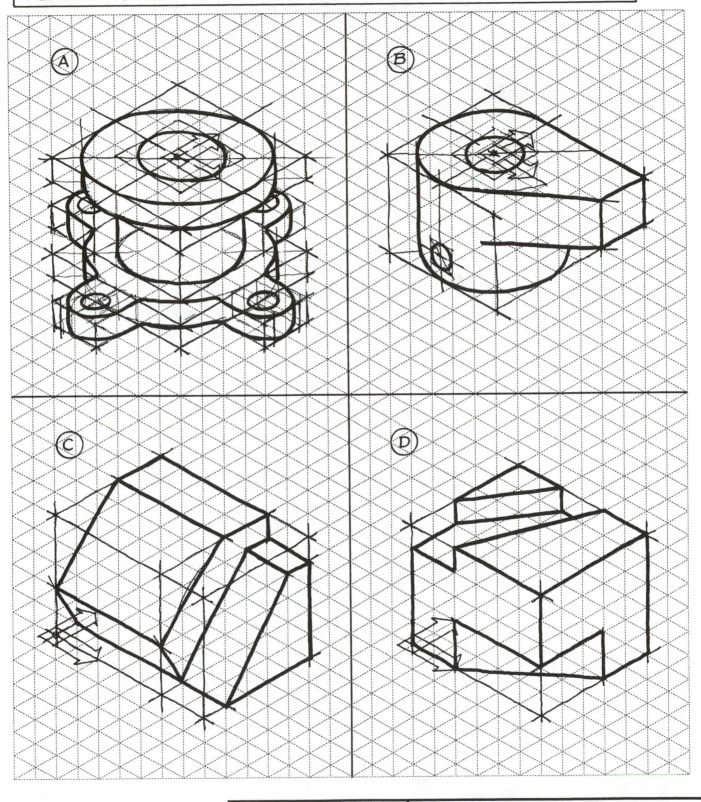

COMPLETE THREE-VIEW ORTHOGRAPHIC SKETCHES OF THE FOLLOWING OBJECTS. USE ORTHO GRID PAPER.

Drawn By:		FREEHAND SKETCHING	
	Scale	TITLE PICTORIAL OBJECTS	
Date	Sheet of	Drawing Number A	2.6

QUESTIONS:

1. What is the name of the object?

2. What line represents surface (G) in the top view?

3. What is dimension (J)?

4. What is the total width of the part as shown by dimension (A)?

5. What is the radius of rounded end (R)?

6. From what type of material is the part made?

7. What is the size of dimension (C)?

8. Which line in the top view is used to represent surface (K) in the right side view?

9. What type of line is (D)?

10. What type of line is (M)?

ANSWERS:

1. _____

2. _____

3. _____

4. _____

5. _____

6. _____

7. _____

8. _____

9. _____

10. _____

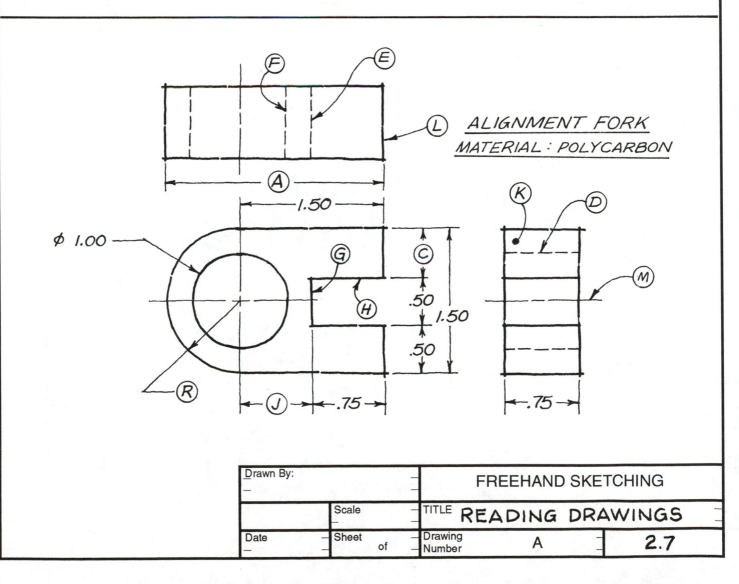

ALIGNMENT FORK
MATERIAL : POLYCARBON

Drawn By:		FREEHAND SKETCHING	
	Scale	TITLE READING DRAWINGS	
Date	Sheet of	Drawing Number	A 2.7

3 Isometric Sketching

Isometric Views — General Conditions

An *isometric view* (iso meaning equal, metric meaning measure) displays three sides of an object in a *pictorial* view. The three sides may be top, front, and one side, or any other combination of three mutually perpendicular faces (Fig 3-1). Note that one view presents the isometric in a different orientation.

An isometric view displays the three faces in equal inclination and scale. Measurements can be made along or parallel to any of the isometric axes. These axes are set at 30, 90, and 150 degrees. Measurements cannot be made at any other angle (Fig. 3-2).

Isometric sketches usually don't include hidden features by means of hidden lines.

A true isometric projection equally foreshortens measurements along the axes to 82%. To make construction simple, the usual practice in isometric drawing is to measure along isometric axes at full scale. This produces a correctly proportioned, but slightly larger view.

Sheet 3.0 on page 47 shows the steps in making an isometric sketch. The overall height, width, and depth are noted as distances D1, D2, and D3.

Step 1 Place the most descriptive orientation to the front so that an appropriate side is shown. Construct the overall shape of the object using D1, D2, and D3. This is called the *boxing-out* construction method.

Step 2 Locate the edges and surfaces by measuring parallel to the isometric axes.

Step 3 Complete the pictorial by darkening the visible edges and surfaces.

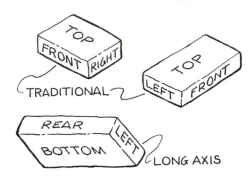

Fig. 3-1. Arrangement of isometric views.

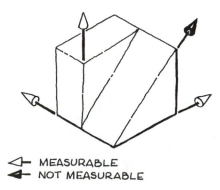

MEASURABLE
NOT MEASURABLE

Fig. 3-2. Valid measurement directions in isometric.

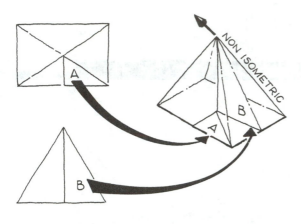

Fig. 3-3. Offset method of constructing nonisometric lines.

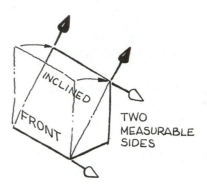

Fig. 3-4. Inclined plane in isometric.

Isometric and Nonisometric Lines

An isometric line is any line parallel to one of the isometric axes. A nonisometric line is any line not parallel to an isometric axis. Isometric lines can be measured directly. Nonisometric lines must be found by measuring the components of the right triangle of which the nonisometric line is the hypotenuse (Fig. 3-3). This is called the *offset method* of construction.

Inclined and Oblique Planes

An inclined plane (Fig. 3-4) may be considered an isometric plane revolved about one of the isometric axes. Its edges are nonisometric lines and must be found as such. Note that two edges of an inclined plane are isometric lines and can be measured directly.

An oblique plane has been rotated about two isometric axes (Fig 3-5). This results in all boundary lines being nonisometric. You cannot measure directly on an oblique plane.

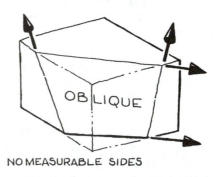

Fig. 3-5. Oblique plane by offset construction.

Angles in Isometric

Because an angle other than a multiple of 90° creates a nonisometric line, it is found by the offset method. Sometimes, sketching the angle first orthographically and then transfering the right triangle legs into isometric is easiest (Fig. 3-6).

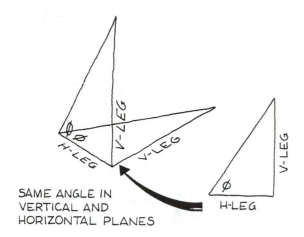

Fig. 3-6. An angle in isometric.

Circular Features

The general method for sketching any curve in isometric is a modified offset method — *grid construction*. Both circular and noncircular curves can be done this way (Fig. 3-7). Irregular curves require a grid with divisions fine enough to produce a sufficient number of control points that the curve can be plotted. Sketching circles involves the use of a simplified example of the grid method where the shape is boxed out to find the axes and tangent points (Fig. 3-8).

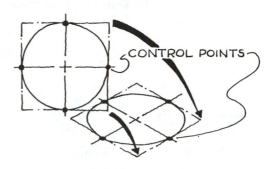

Fig. 3-8. Circular construction by boxing out.

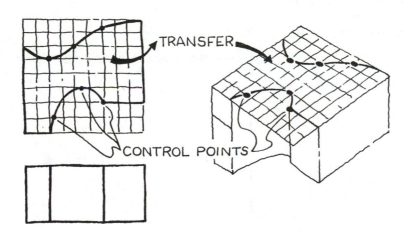

Fig. 3-7. Grid method of constructing curves.

Practical Example

In Fig. 3-9 three orthographic views of an object having circular and inclined features are shown. This solution requires the following steps:

1. Decide on the orientation for a front isometric face.

2. Box out the overall dimensions of height, width, and depth.

3. Locate inclined surfaces by the offset method.

4. Locate the center of circular features. Find their center lines and box out the general shape.

5. Complete the line work to show complete visibility.

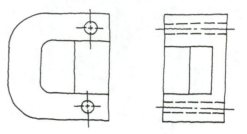

CAD Example — 2D

The same sketching techniques of boxing out, offset, and grid construction can be applied using 2D CAD tools. Some of these tools automate construction at isometric angles (30°, 90°, 150°) and the angle and exposure of isometric circles (Fig. 3-10).

CAD Example — 3D

An isometric *projection* can be achieved by either rotating the object or moving the viewer. In Fig. 3-11, note that the front view axis system has remained in place, signifying that the viewer has taken a viewing position at X=1, Y=1, Z=1, looking back at 0, 0, 0.

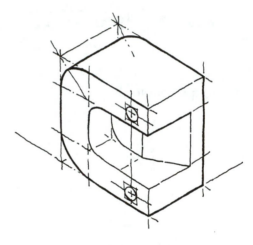

Fig. 3-9. Practical example of an isometric sketch.

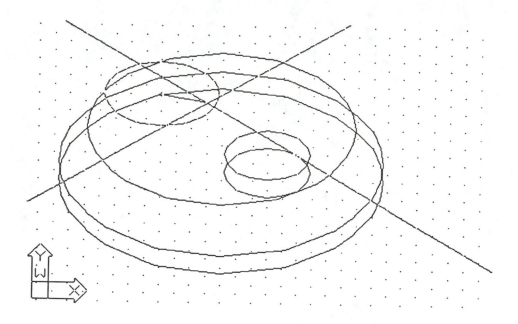

Fig. 3-10. Automated 2D CAD isometric constructions.

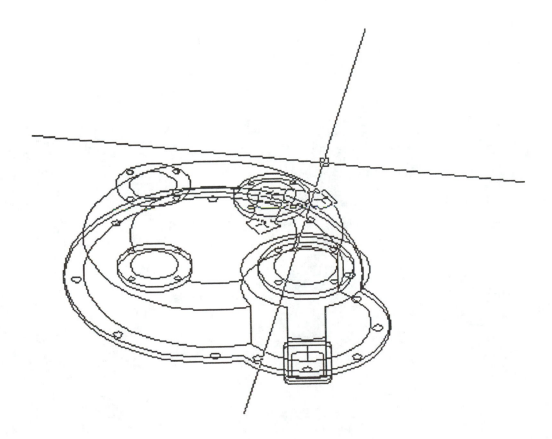

Figure 3-11 Isometric in 3D by viewpoint.

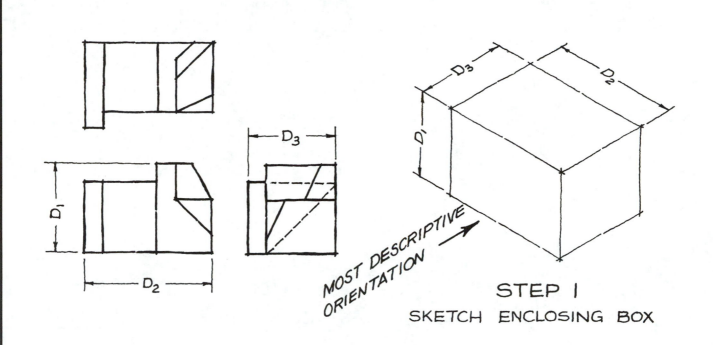

D_3

D_1

D_2

MOST DESCRIPTIVE ORIENTATION

STEP 1
SKETCH ENCLOSING BOX

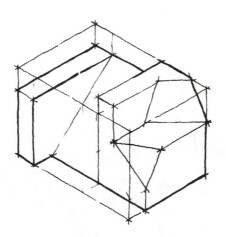

STEP 2
LOCATE EDGES AND SURFACES

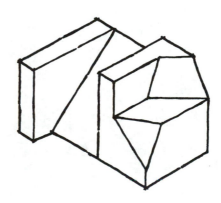

STEP 3
COMPLETE PICTORIAL

STEPS IN MAKING AN ISOMETRIC SKETCH

Drawn By:			FREEHAND SKETCHING		
	Scale		TITLE	SAMPLE	
Date	Sheet of		Drawing Number	A	3.0

COMPLETE AN ISOMETRIC SKETCH OF EACH OBJECT. SHADE INCLINED AND OBLIQUE PLANES AS ASSIGNED.

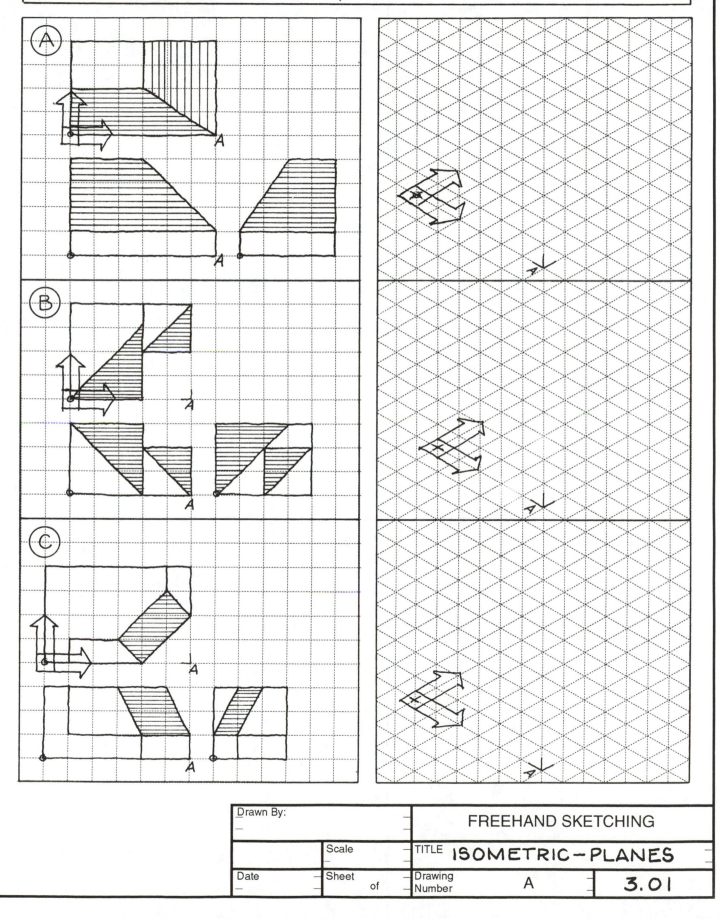

A

B

C

Drawn By:		FREEHAND SKETCHING		
	Scale	TITLE ISOMETRIC - PLANES		
Date	Sheet of	Drawing Number	A	3.01

COMPLETE AN ISOMETRIC SKETCH OF THE FOLLOWING OBJECTS.
CHOOSE THE MOST DESCRIPTIVE FEATURE. USE ISO GRID PAPER.

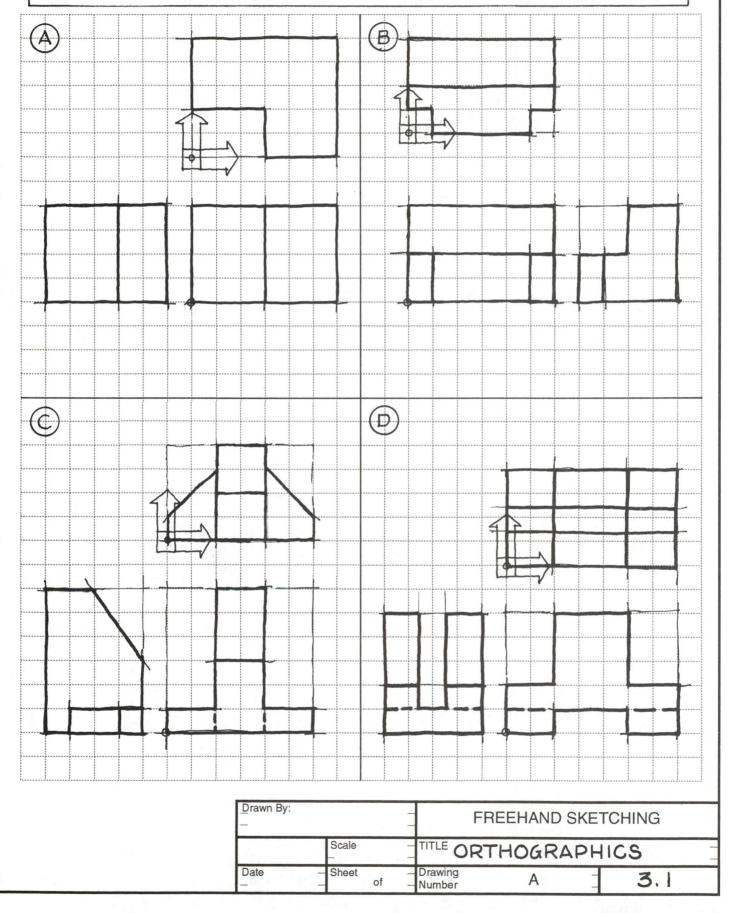

Drawn By:			FREEHAND SKETCHING		
	Scale		TITLE ORTHOGRAPHICS		
Date	Sheet	of	Drawing Number	A	3.1

COMPLETE AN ISOMETRIC SKETCH OF THE FOLLOWING OBJECTS. CHOOSE THE MOST DESCRIPTIVE ORIENTATION. USE ISO GRID PAPER.

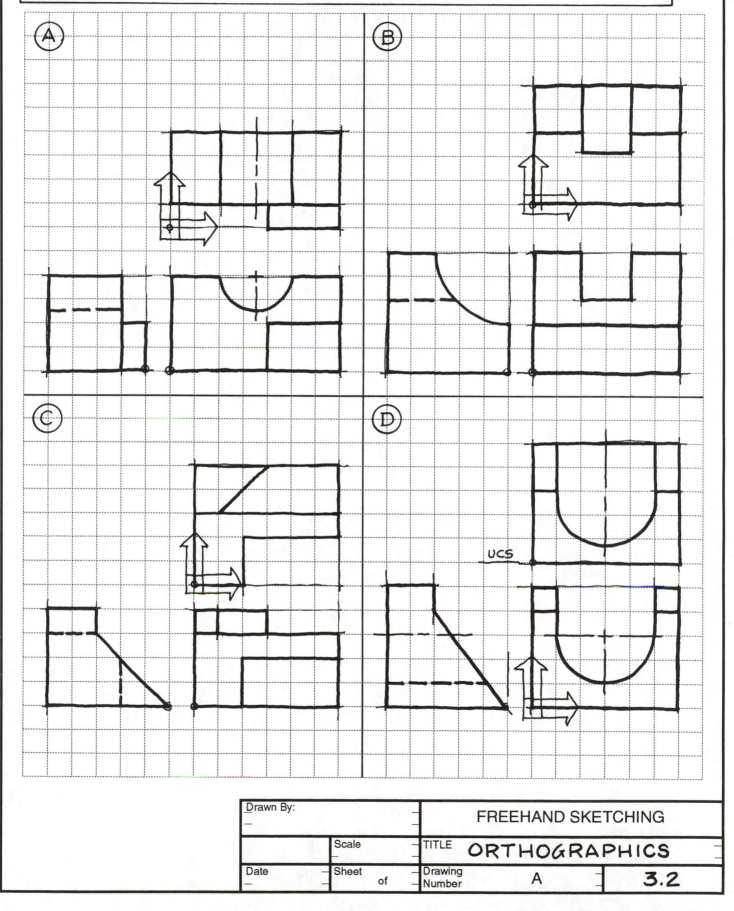

Drawn By:		FREEHAND SKETCHING		
	Scale	TITLE **ORTHOGRAPHICS**		
Date	Sheet of	Drawing Number	A	**3.2**

COMPLETE AN ISOMETRIC SKETCH OF THE FOLLOWING OBJECTS. CHOOSE THE MOST DESCRIPTIVE ORIENTATION. USE ISO GRID PAPER.

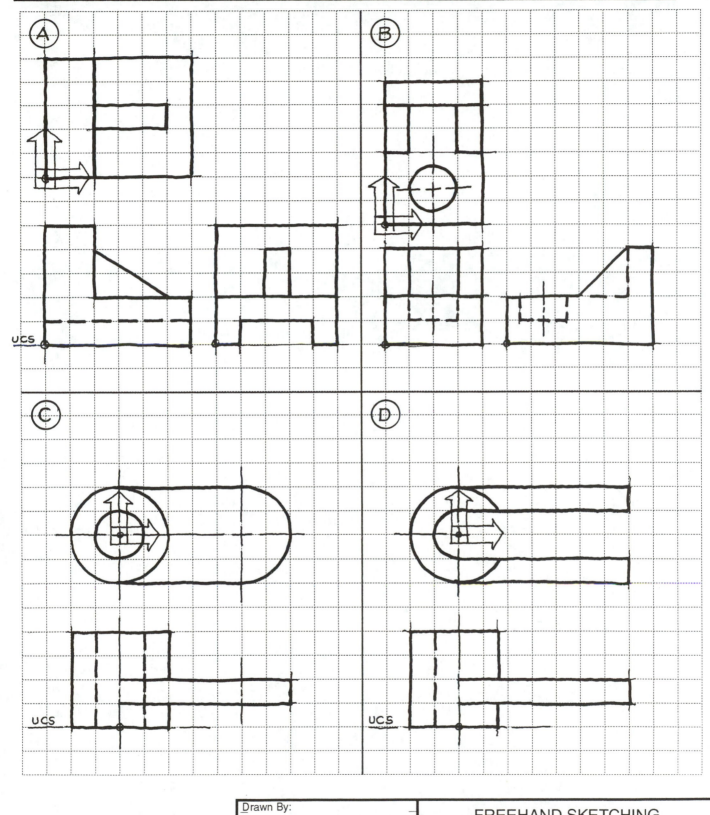

A

B

C

D

UCS

Drawn By:			FREEHAND SKETCHING		
	Scale		TITLE ORTHOGRAPHICS		
Date	Sheet	of	Drawing Number	A	3.3

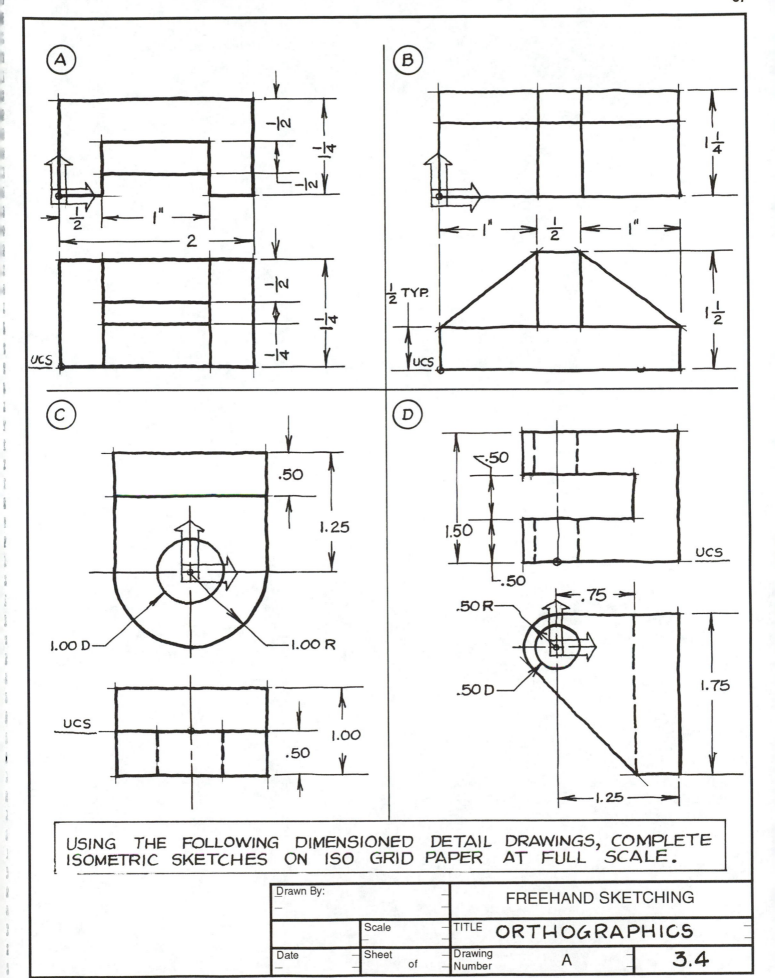

USING THE FOLLOWING DIMENSIONED DETAIL DRAWINGS, COMPLETE
ISOMETRIC SKETCHES ON ISO GRID PAPER AT FULL SCALE.

Drawn By:			FREEHAND SKETCHING		
	Scale		TITLE **ORTHOGRAPHICS**		
Date	Sheet of		Drawing Number	A	**3.4**

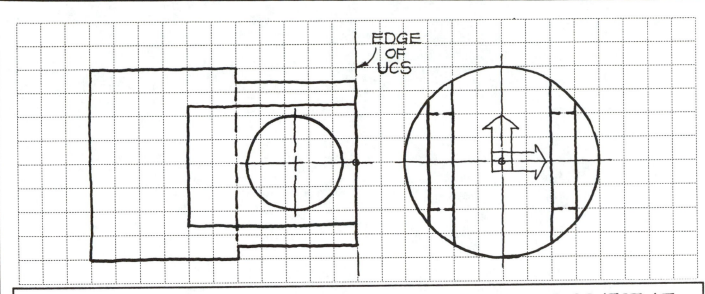

EDGE
OF
UCS

COMPLETE AN ISOMETRIC SKETCH OF THE FOLLOWING OBJECT AT FULL SCALE. CHOOSE THE MOST DESCRIPTIVE ORIENTATION.

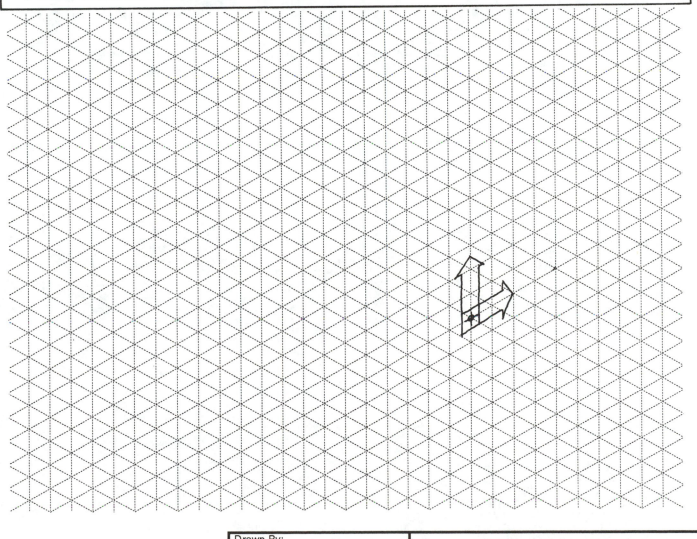

Drawn By:		FREEHAND SKETCHING		
	Scale	TITLE ISOMETRIC SKETCH		
Date	Sheet of	Drawing Number	A	3.5

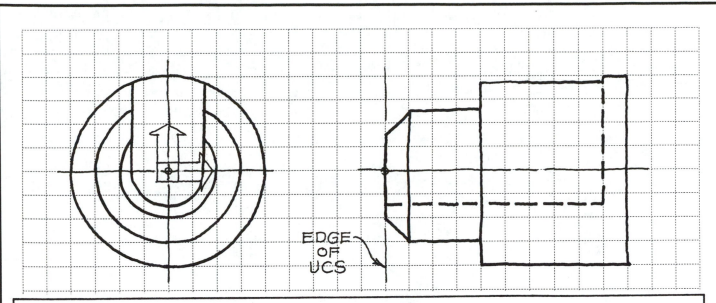

EDGE
OF
UCS

COMPLETE AN ISOMETRIC SKETCH OF THE FOLLOWING OBJECT AT FULL SCALE. CHOOSE THE MOST DESCRIPTIVE ORIENTATION.

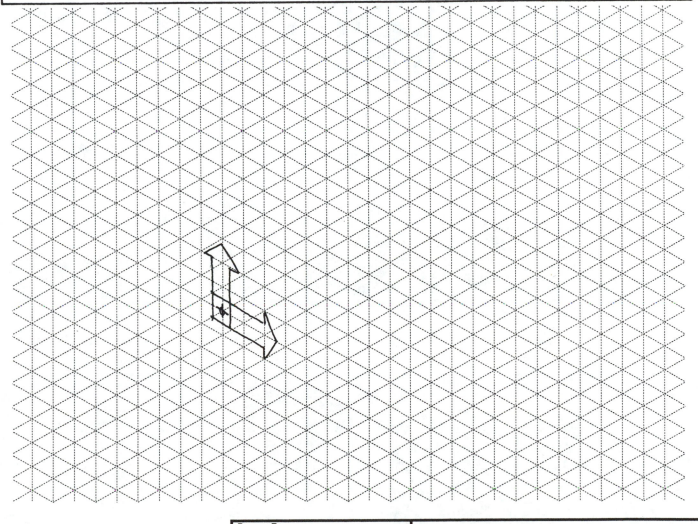

Drawn By:		FREEHAND SKETCHING		
	Scale	TITLE ISOMETRIC SKETCH		
Date	Sheet of	Drawing Number	A	3.6

COMPLETE AN ISOMETRIC SKETCH OF THE FOLLOWING OBJECT AT THE SAME SCALE (1:1). USE ISO GRID PAPER.

EDGE OF UCS

Drawn By:			FREEHAND SKETCHING		
	Scale		TITLE VIEWS FOR ISOMETRIC		
Date	Sheet of	Drawing Number	A		3.7

4 Orthographic Reading

Orthographic Reading — General Conditions

Orthographic views may be read much like a written language. When you read a view, you interpret lines to form a mental picture of what the object looks like. To fully understand an object's geometry from only one view is difficult. When two or more orthogonal views are arranged in close proximity, you can glance from one view to the next, mentally noting a feature's position and shape, and in doing so, become familiar with its shape. This process is called *reading the views*.

Understanding the relationship of views and positions in space is important. In Fig. 4-1, note the position of the block on top of the object in each view. It is on the right rear of the object in each view. To be able to read the views, you need to be able to communicate where you are in space and in which way you are moving.

Reading is an activity that makes you a better sketcher. Interestingly, the better pictorial sketcher you are, the better you can solve reading problems. For that reason, we presented pictorial sketching first.

Understanding Surfaces

The position of a surface determines how it will appear in orthographic views. In general, a plane can appear in true shape, as an edge, or in infinitely many foreshortened positions. There are two unchangeable truths about planes:

Truth 1 The basic shape of a plane doesn't change view to view. A circular plane appears as a circle, ellipse, or line; a square plane appears as a square, parallelogram, or line; a triangular plane appears as a triangle, a smaller triangle, or a line (Fig. 4-2).

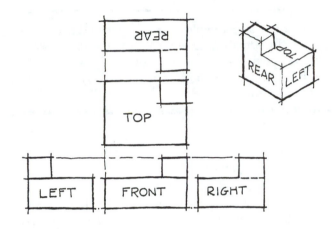

Fig. 4-1. Spatial interpretation of two-dimensional views.

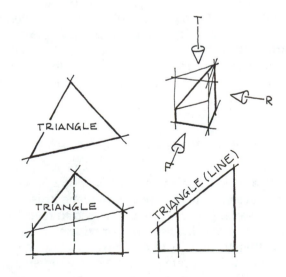

Fig. 4-2. Basic shape of a plane can't be changed.

Truth 2 The height, width, and depth of a plane relative to a stable axis system doesn't change. If a plane is 2" above the base in the front view, it will be 2" above the base in the side view because both views show true height (Fig. 4-3).

Sheet 4.0 (page 69) presents a pictorial view and top, front, and right side views of an object with many surfaces. Note how much easier it is to visualize the orthographic views when the pictorial is present.

A plane can be perpendicular to one of the directions of sight for a principal view — top, front, or right side. These planes are called *horizontal*, *frontal*, and *profile*. If a plane is parallel to only one direction, it is said to be *inclined*. If a plane is at an angle to all principal directions of sight, it is said to be *oblique*.

Assignment: Using the pictorial on Sheet 4.0 as a guide, assign the correct labels to the planes in the top, front, and right side views. Use arrows where necessary. Using the definitions, complete boxes A–L in appropriate technical lettering.

Reading Exercises

When you read views, you generally are trying to find information already on the view or complete a new view. A technique that helps you find information is the use of a *reference plane*. Figure 4-4 shows an object in the front and top views. Assume that you want to sketch the right side view. Note that a plane of reference has been installed at the front of the object in the top view, controlling all depth measurements. The same reference plane appears as an edge in the side view. Depth measurements in the side view will be identical to their corresponding depth measurements in the top view. Height information is obtained from the front view.

Use of Cutting Plane

Similar to a reference plane is a *cutting plane*. The difference lies in its use. A reference plane is used to measure, whereas a cutting plane is used to reveal intersections. These intersections provide common points so that geometry can be drawn. A cutting plane is normally used to locate points on curved intersections as shown in Fig. 4-5. As with a reference plane, the cutting plane should be passed perpendicular (normal) to some line of sight. Figure 4-6 shows two

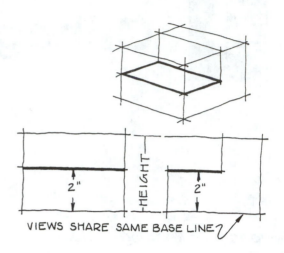

Fig. 4-3. Position in space can't be changed.

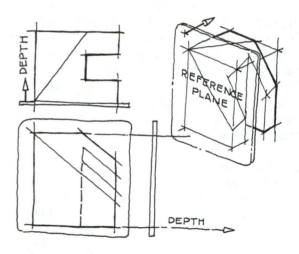

Fig. 4-4. Use of reference plane. See also Sheet 4.8.

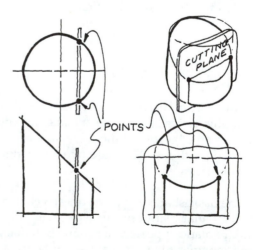

Fig. 4-5. Use of cutting plane.

cutting planes that have been passed in the front view to locate the same points. The horizontal cutting plane is perpendicular to the top direction of sight. The vertical cutting plane is perpendicular to the side view line of sight.

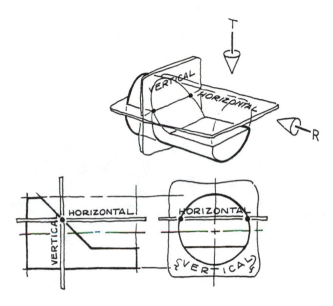

Fig 4-6. Position of reference normal to line of sight.

Practical Example

In Fig. 4-7 front and right side views of a cylindrical object are shown. You are required to create a top view.

1. Sketch a general shape that describes the overall width (from the front view) and depth (from the side view).

2. Pass a plane of reference vertically through the cylinder in the side view. This appears as a horizontal line in the top view.

3. In the side view, locate the general feature depth perpendicular to this reference.

4. Find the corresponding points in the front view. Transfer the depth of these limits to the front view and project to the top view.

5. Locate the limits of the curve in the side view. Transfer these limits to the front view and project to the top view.

6. Transfer the depth measurements for these limits from the side view to the top view using the reference plane.

7. Pass cutting planes in the side view to locate intermediate points along the curve between the limits.

8. Find these intermediate points in the front view.

9. Locate the cutting planes in the top view by measuring their distances from the reference plane.

10. Complete the curve and then complete the entire view.

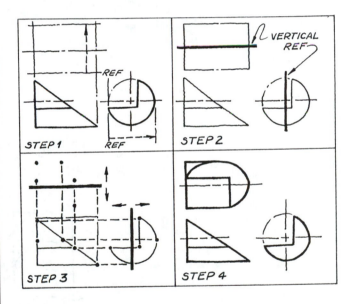

Fig. 4-7. Solution of orthographic views.

CAD Example — 2D

CAD systems automate the two-dimensional constructions previously described. Because software will report dictances very accurately, new views can be rapidly constructed.

CAD Example — 3D

With a three-dimensional model, *any* view is possible. The technique is similar to that of a reference plane and is often called a *construction plane*. A construction plane may be set at any position and at any orientation in space. A viewing position taken perpendicular to this plane results in a view of the objects as if it were projected onto the plane. Figure 4-8 shows an object with construction plane (UCS) icon in place and the view seen looking perpendicular to that plane.

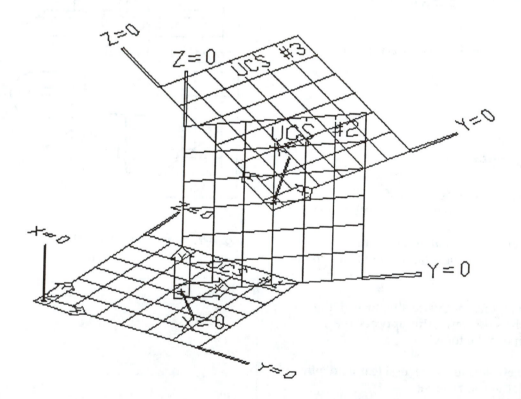

Fig 4-8. Views in 3D CAD generated by placement of construction planes.

1. Label the surfaces and edges on the orthographic multiviews to match the letters shown on the isometric pictorial.

2. Complete the table below by identifying each type of surface. Shade ALL surfaces on the multiview and the isometric pictorial drawing as follows.

SURFACE Identification and Definition	Color
FRONTAL: A normal surface or plane parallel to the front of an object.	Red
HORIZONTAL: A normal surface or plane parallel to the top of an object.	Green
PROFILE: A normal surface or plane parallel to the right side of an object.	Blue
INCLINED: A surface or plane sloped at one angle that it appears as foreshortened in two of the principal views of an object and as an edge in the third view.	Yellow
OBLIQUE: A surface or plane sloped at two angles so that it appears as foreshortened in all three principal views of an object.	Orange

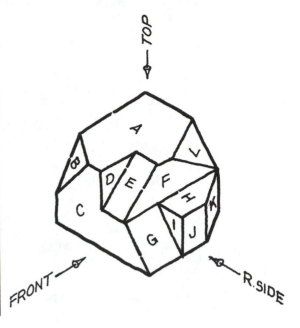

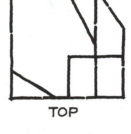

TOP

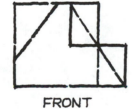

FRONT

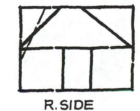

R. SIDE

A		G	
B		H	
C		I	
D		J	
E		K	
F		L	

Drawn By:		FREEHAND SKETCHING	
	Scale	TITLE **READING SURFACES**	
Date	Sheet of	Drawing Number	A	4.0

71

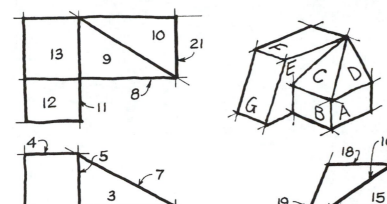

IN THE TABLES, LIST THE NUMBERS CORRESPONDING TO THE LETTERS.

EXAMPLE →

	Top	Front	Side
A	21	6	14
B			
C			
D			
E			
F			
G			

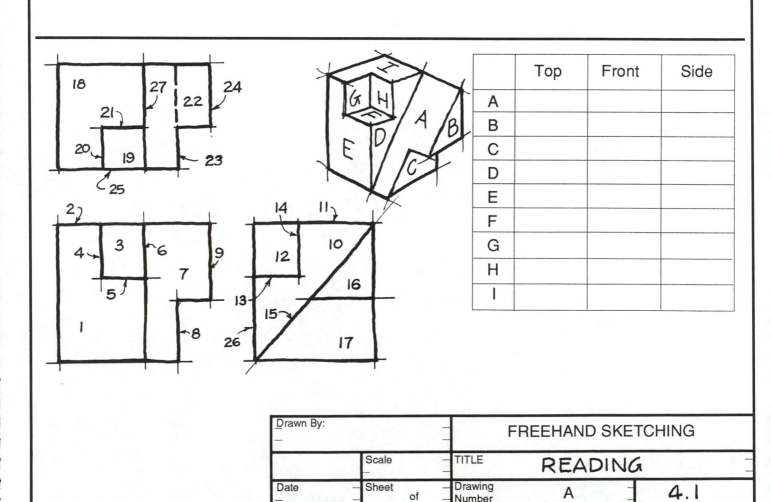

	Top	Front	Side
A			
B			
C			
D			
E			
F			
G			
H			
I			

Drawn By:

Scale

Date   Sheet   of

FREEHAND SKETCHING

TITLE   READING

Drawing Number   A   4.1

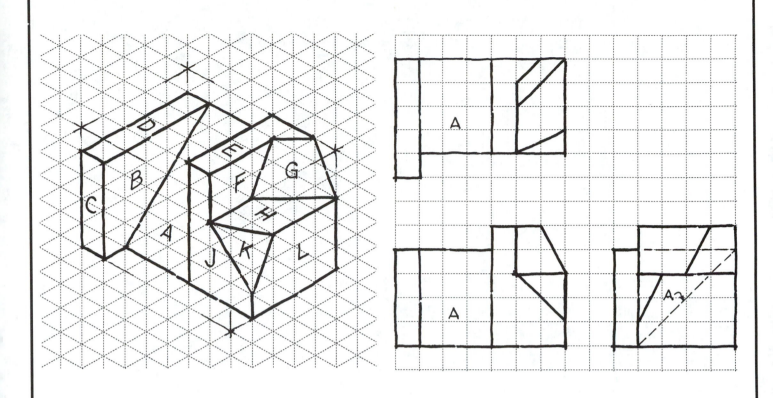

SURFACE IDENTIFICATION: Using the following descriptions, complete the table as shown in the example.

1 = TRUE SHAPE: When a surface is perpendicular to your line of sight in a given orthographic view, the surface is refered to as true shape.

2 = LINE: In an orthographic view, the edge view of a surface is represented by a line. The direction of the surface is therefore parallel to your line of sight in that view.

3 = FORESHORTENED: When a surface is sloped at an angle so that it is neither parallel nor perpendicular to your line of sight in a principal view, the surface is refered to as foreshortened.

EXAMPLE

ISO	TOP	FRONT	R.SIDE
A	3	3	2
B			
C			
D			
E			
F			
G			
H			
J			
K			
L			

Drawn By:		FREEHAND SKETCHING	
	Scale	TITLE READING	
Date	Sheet of	Drawing Number A	4.2

COMPLETE THE MISSING VIEW OF EACH SINGLE SOLID OBJECT.

Drawn By:		FREEHAND SKETCHING	
	Scale	TITLE MISSING VIEWS	
Date	Sheet of	Drawing Number	A	4.3

COMPLETE THE MISSING VIEW OF EACH SINGLE SOLID OBJECT.

Drawn By:		FREEHAND SKETCHING		
	Scale	TITLE	MISSING VIEWS	
Date	Sheet of	Drawing Number	A	4.4

COMPLETE THE MISSING VIEW OF EACH SINGLE SOLID OBJECT.

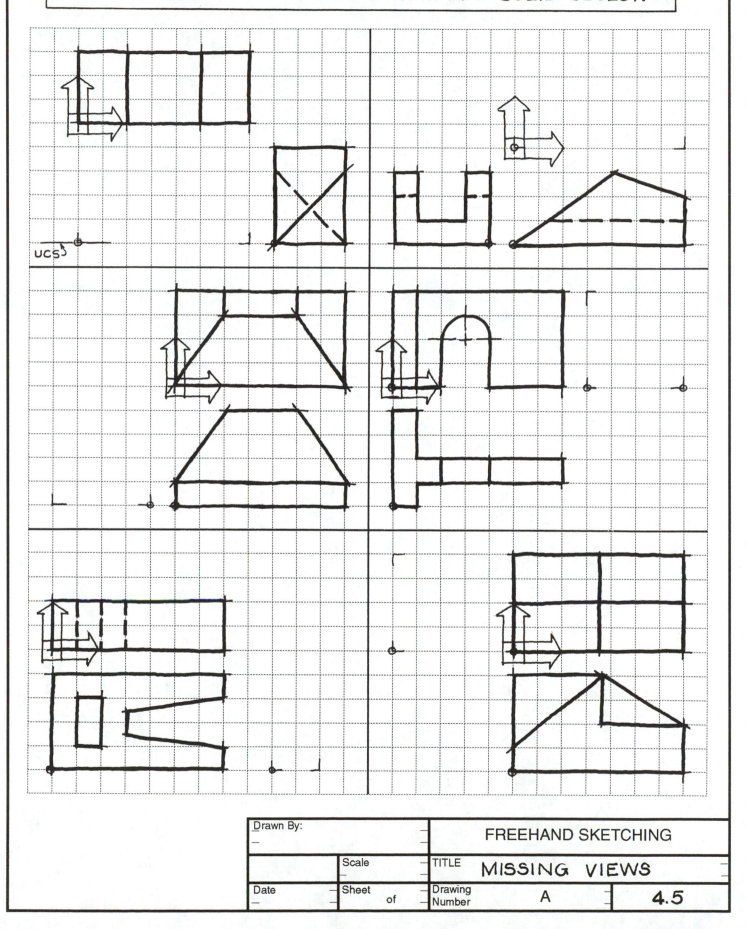

Drawn By:			FREEHAND SKETCHING	
	Scale		TITLE MISSING VIEWS	
Date	Sheet of	Drawing Number	A	4.5

81

COMPLETE THE MISSING VIEW OF EACH SINGLE SOLID OBJECT.

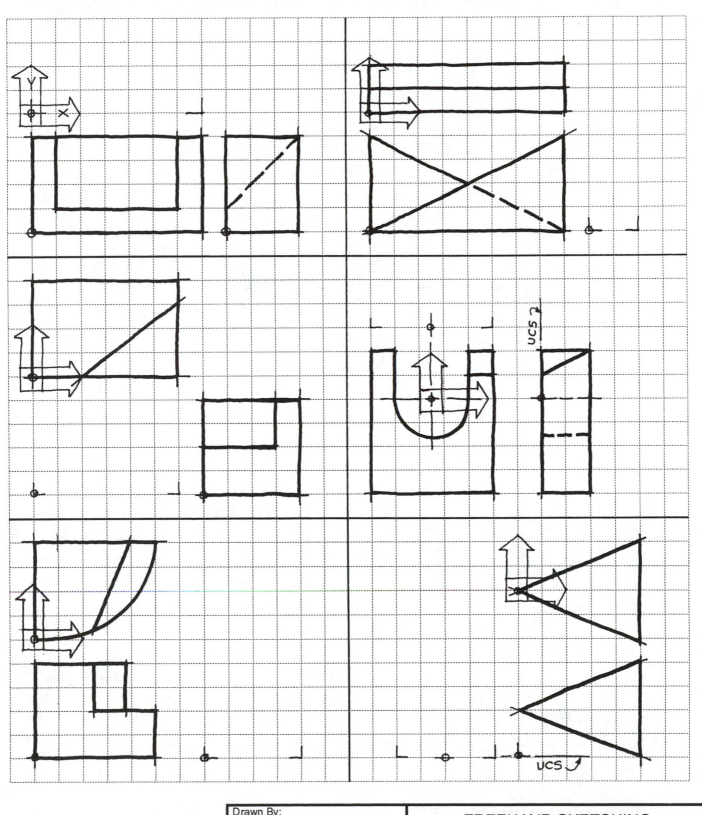

Drawn By:			FREEHAND SKETCHING	
	Scale		TITLE MISSING VIEWS	
Date	Sheet of	Drawing Number	A	4.6

COMPLETE THE MISSING VIEW OF EACH SINGLE SOLID OBJECT.

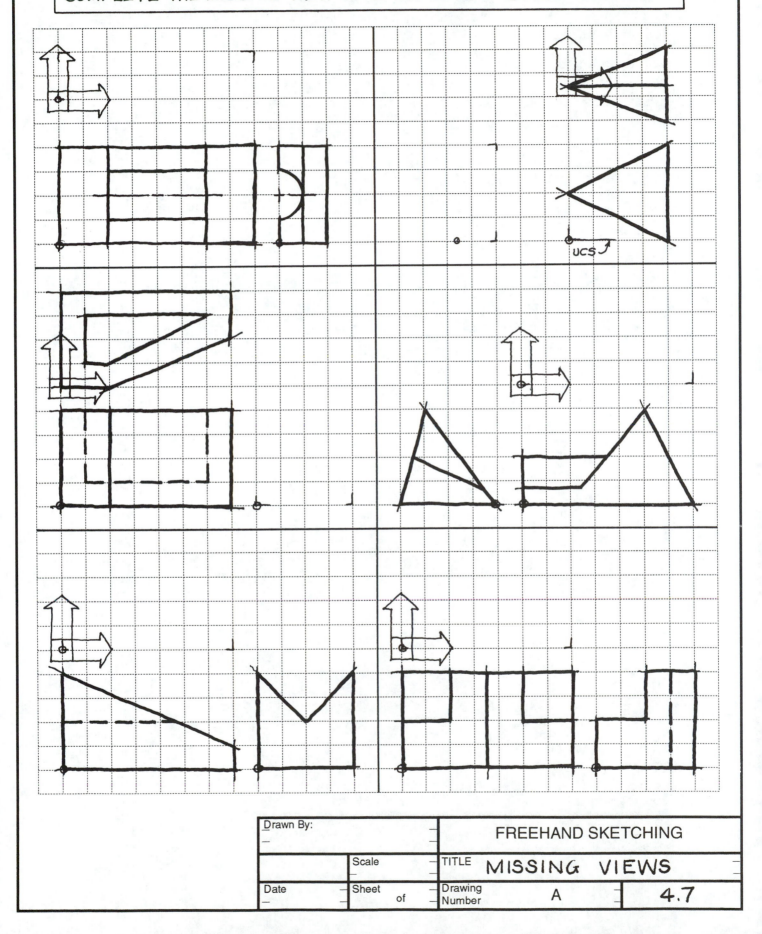

Drawn By:			FREEHAND SKETCHING	
	Scale		TITLE MISSING VIEWS	
Date	Sheet of		Drawing Number	A	4.7

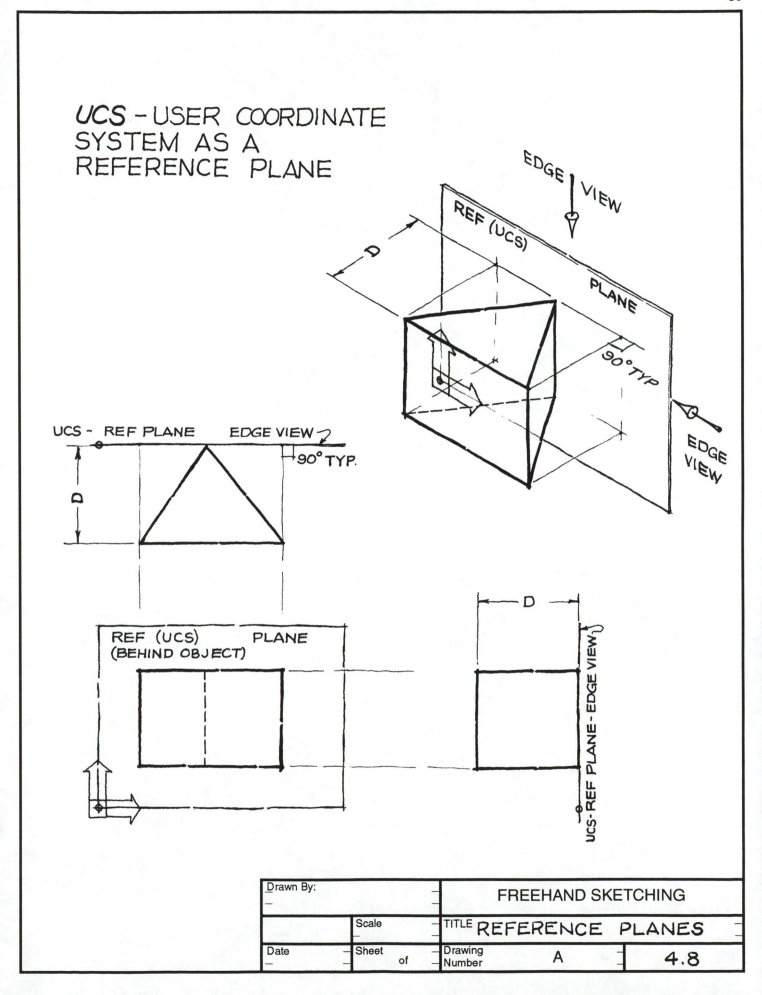

UCS – USER COORDINATE SYSTEM AS A REFERENCE PLANE

REF (UCS) PLANE

EDGE VIEW

D

90° TYP

EDGE VIEW

UCS - REF PLANE   EDGE VIEW

90° TYP.

D

REF (UCS)   PLANE
(BEHIND OBJECT)

D

UCS - REF PLANE - EDGE VIEW

Drawn By:		FREEHAND SKETCHING		
	Scale	TITLE REFERENCE PLANES		
Date	Sheet of	Drawing Number	A	4.8

87

USING A REFERENCE PLANE AS SHOWN IN PROBLEM Ⓐ, SOLVE THE MISSING VIEWS IN ALL OF THE PROBLEMS BELOW.

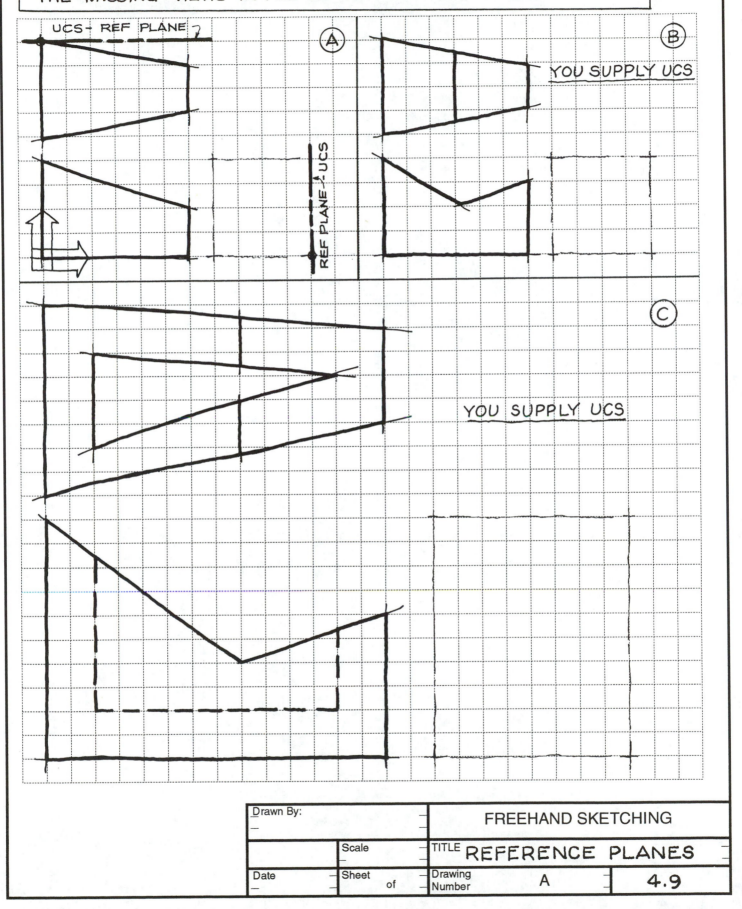

UCS- REF PLANE

Ⓐ

REF PLANE ⊥ UCS

Ⓑ

YOU SUPPLY UCS

Ⓒ

YOU SUPPLY UCS

Drawn By:		FREEHAND SKETCHING		
	Scale	TITLE REFERENCE PLANES		
Date	Sheet of	Drawing Number	A	4.9

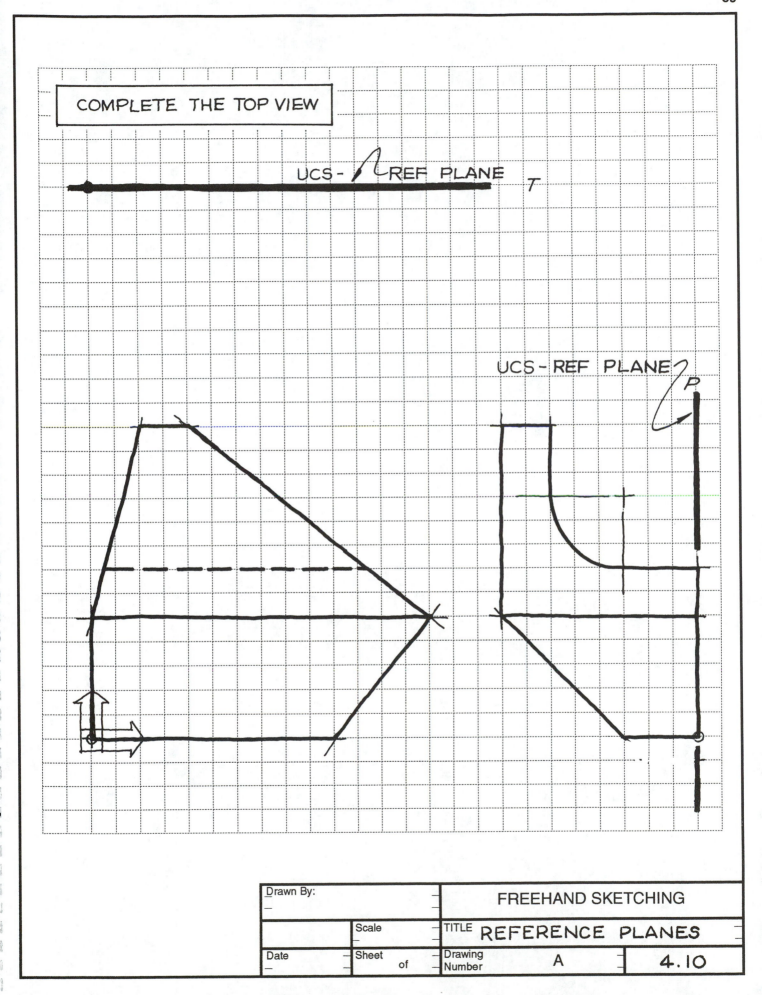

COMPLETE THE TOP VIEW

UCS - REF PLANE   T

UCS - REF PLANE   P

Drawn By:		FREEHAND SKETCHING	
	Scale	TITLE REFERENCE PLANES	
Date	Sheet of	Drawing Number A	4.10

SUPPLY THE MISSING VIEWS.   THE VIEWS THAT ARE GIVEN
ARE CORRECT AND COMPLETE.

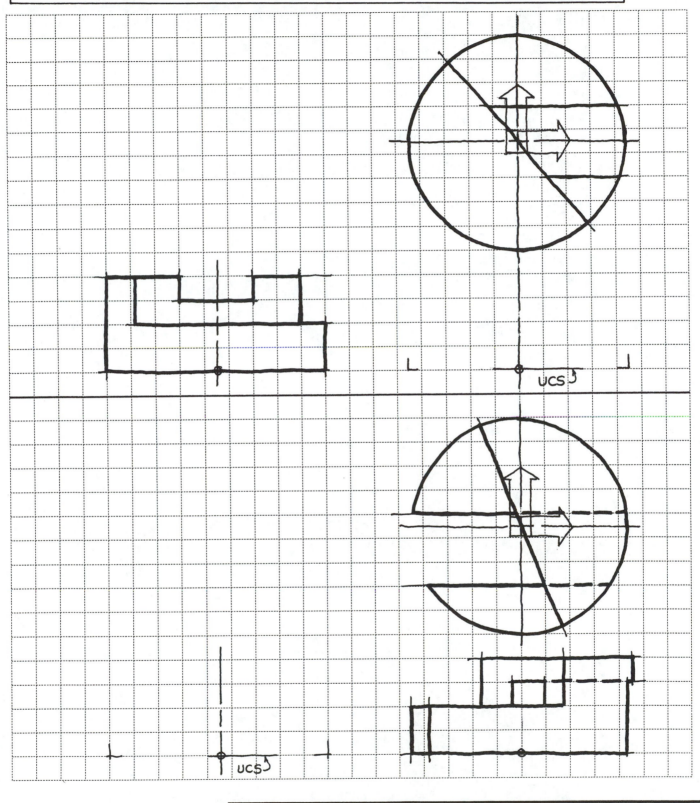

Drawn By:		FREEHAND SKETCHING		
	Scale	TITLE REFERENCE PLANES		
Date	Sheet of	Drawing Number	A	4.11

SUPPLY THE MISSING VIEWS.   THE VIEWS THAT ARE GIVEN
ARE CORRECT AND COMPLETE. USE CUTTING PLANES.

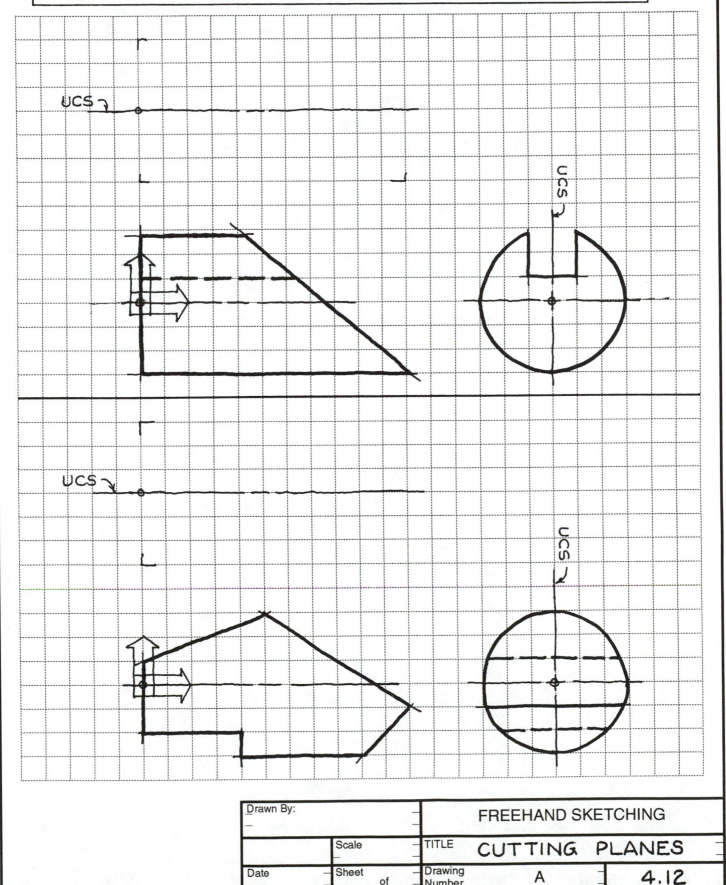

Drawn By:			FREEHAND SKETCHING		
	Scale		TITLE CUTTING PLANES		
Date	Sheet	of	Drawing Number	A	4.12

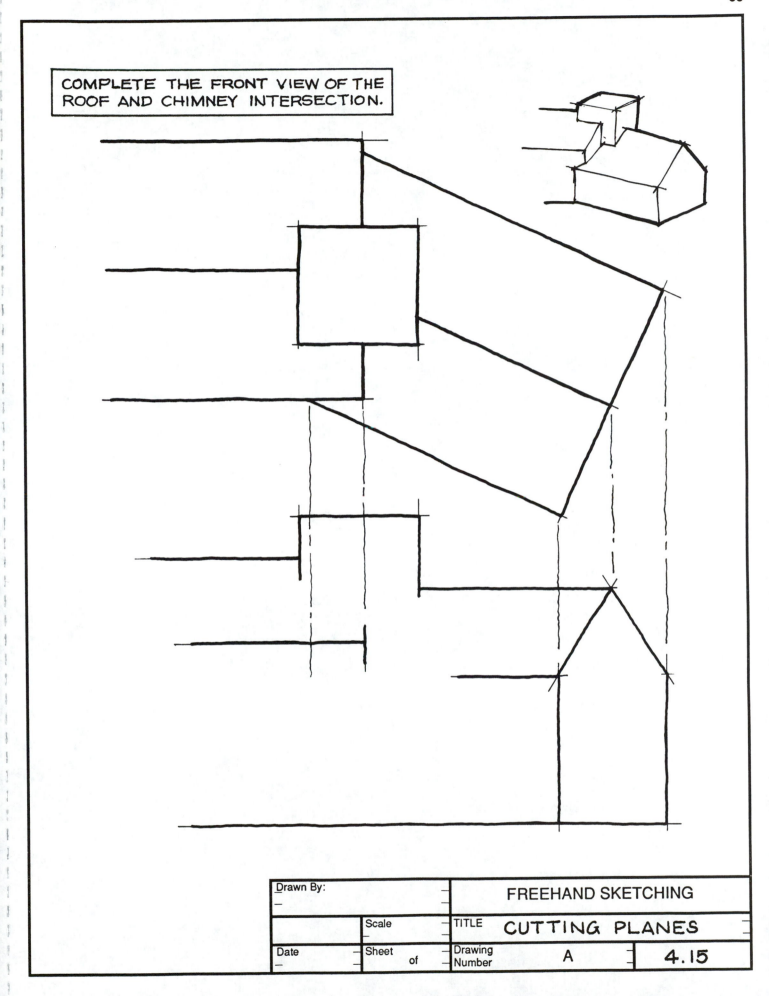

COMPLETE THE FRONT VIEW OF THE
ROOF AND CHIMNEY INTERSECTION.

Drawn By:			FREEHAND SKETCHING	
	Scale		TITLE CUTTING PLANES	
Date	Sheet of		Drawing Number A	4.15

QUESTIONS:

1. Surface (C) in the top view appears as an edge in which view?

2. Surface (A) in the front view is shown as what surface in the top view?

3. What type of surface is (J)?

4. What material is the tool block made of?

5. How many inclined surfaces can be found on the tool block?

6. How many profile surfaces are on the block?

7. Surface (P) is what type of surface?

8. How many oblique surfaces can be found on the tool block?

9. Is surface (B) parallel to surface (O)?

10. Is surface (J) parallel to surface (G)?

ANSWERS:

1. _____

2. _____

3. _____

4. _____

5. _____

6. _____

7. _____

8. _____

9. _____

10. _____

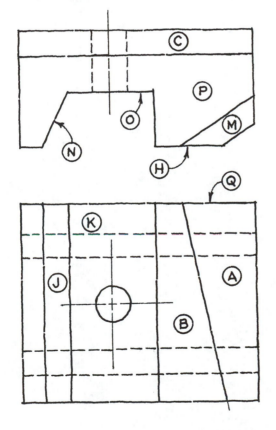

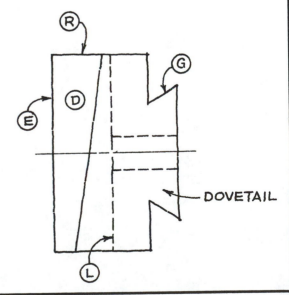

TOOL BLOCK

DOVETAIL

Drawn By:		FREEHAND SKETCHING	
	Scale	TITLE READING DRAWINGS	
Date	Sheet of	Drawing Number A	4.16

5 Auxiliary Views

Auxiliary Views — General Conditions

An *auxiliary view* is a view taken at an angle that is not parallel to an object's axis system. For example, the view marked A1 in Fig. 5-1 is parallel to the object's Y axis but at an angle to UCS-Z and UCS-X. An auxiliary viewing position is taken to

1. facilitate the construction of geometry not perpendicular or parallel to the object's axis system,

2. display angular or oblique geometry in normal position, and.

3. display the object in pictorial position.

Note in Fig. 5-1 that view A1 establishes an view axis system normal to its X–Z directions. Taking a correct viewing direction is the first and most important step in achieving an auxiliary view. **The view is defined by the direction of sight.** Auxiliary views are drawn so that measurements can be made, angles determined, and clearances found. Because much geometry in an auxiliary view ends up being foreshortened, *partial auxiliary views*, like that shown in Fig. 5-2, are common.

Sheet 5.0 (page 107) shows the basic relationships in an auxiliary view. Fundamental in is the use of a plane of reference to control spatial measurements perpendicular to the direction of sight. Study the placement of the plane on sheet 5.0 and its appearance relative to the direction of sight in central, adjacent, and related views. In all views, the plane of reference is parallel to the direction of sight for the auxiliary view.

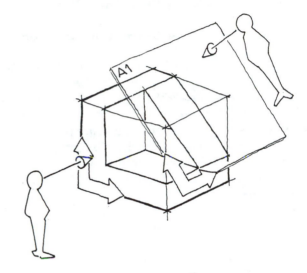

Fig. 5-1. The direction of sight determines the view.

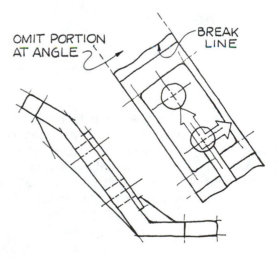

Fig. 5-2. Partial auxiliary view.

Primary and Secondary Auxiliary Views

A *primary auxiliary view* is one where the direction of sight is perpendicular to one of the object's axes and at an angle to the other two.

A *secondary auxiliary view* is one where the direction of sight is at an angle to all three principal object axes (Fig. 5-3).

Assignment: Complete sheet 5.1. Use your main graphics text as a reference to determine definitions. In labeling the views, place labels in the order they are encountered spatially: nearest point to farthest, and farthest point last.

Understanding Auxiliaries

Lines (edges, limits, and intersections) that are parallel to a plane of reference remain parallel to that plane in any and all views. This allows auxiliary views to be easily drawn. Note in Fig. 5-4 that the top and bottom of the object are parallel to the reference plane as revealed in the front view. In the auxiliary view the top and bottom remain parallel to the reference plane.

Not only are the corners parallel, but their distances perpendicular to the reference plane remain constant in all views. These distances are measurable in any view where the reference plane appears as an edge.

Practical Example

Figure 5-5 presents the steps in creating an auxiliary view. In this example, a normal view of the inclined surface is desired.

Step 1. Establish a viewing direction perpendicular to the inclined surface. This can be done in the side view where the inclined surface appears as an edge. The plane of reference that controls spatial measurements is parallel to the direction of sight. It appears normally in the side view and as an edge in the front and top views.

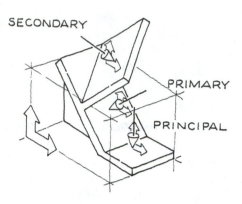

Fig. 5-3. Primary and secondary auxillary views.

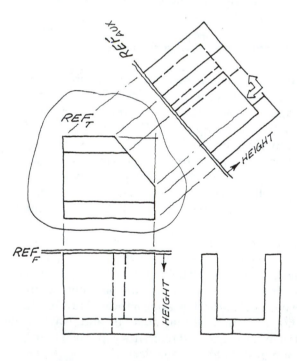

Fig. 5-4. Parallelism in auxiliary views.

Step 2. Establish the edge views of the reference plane in the front and auxiliary views at a convenient width location. You now have three successive views of the reference plane: edge–normal–edge.

Step 3. Project points and vertices into the auxiliary view parallel to the direction of sight.

Step 4. Measure distances perpendicular to the reference in the front view. Lay these measurements off along their corresponding projectors in the auxiliary view, always measuring from the reference plane. Note: Measure in the same direction relative to the central view.

Step 5. Assemble the object in the auxiliary view from near to far, determining visibility as you go.

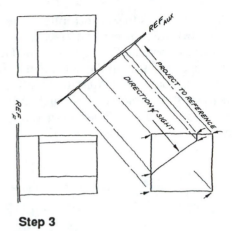

Step 3

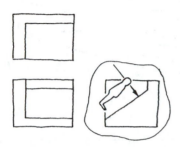

Step 1

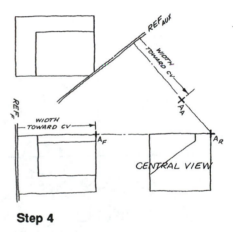

Step 4

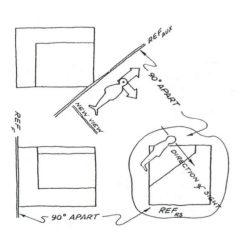

Step 2

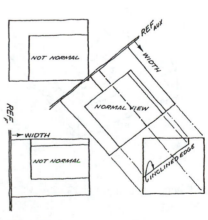

Step 5

Fig. 5-5. Steps in completing an auxiliary view.

CAD Example

The same techniques just discussed to sketch auxiliaries are used in 2D CAD with the addition of CAD's unique tools. Parallel lines can be created through points or at a user-specified perpendicular distance from a base line. Distances can be measured.

Modeling in 3D CAD offers the opportunity to view the geometry directly from any direction. Viewing directions are usually specified in the direction of a vector or normal to a surface., In Fig. 5-6, an oblique surface defines a new view. Note that the UCS is placed on the oblique plane, ensuring that constructions will be normal to that surface. Figure 5-7 has aligned the view to the UCS so that the surface appears normally.

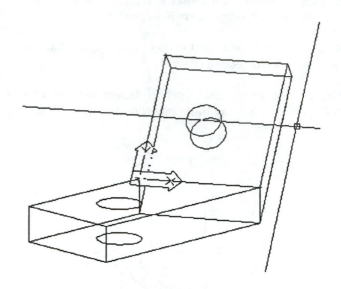

Fig. 5-6. Position of UCS normal to an oblique plane.

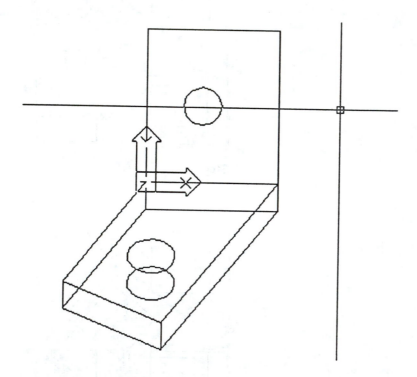

Fig. 5-7. View in Z direction of oblique UCS.

AUXILIARY VIEW
REFERENCE PLANE
METHOD

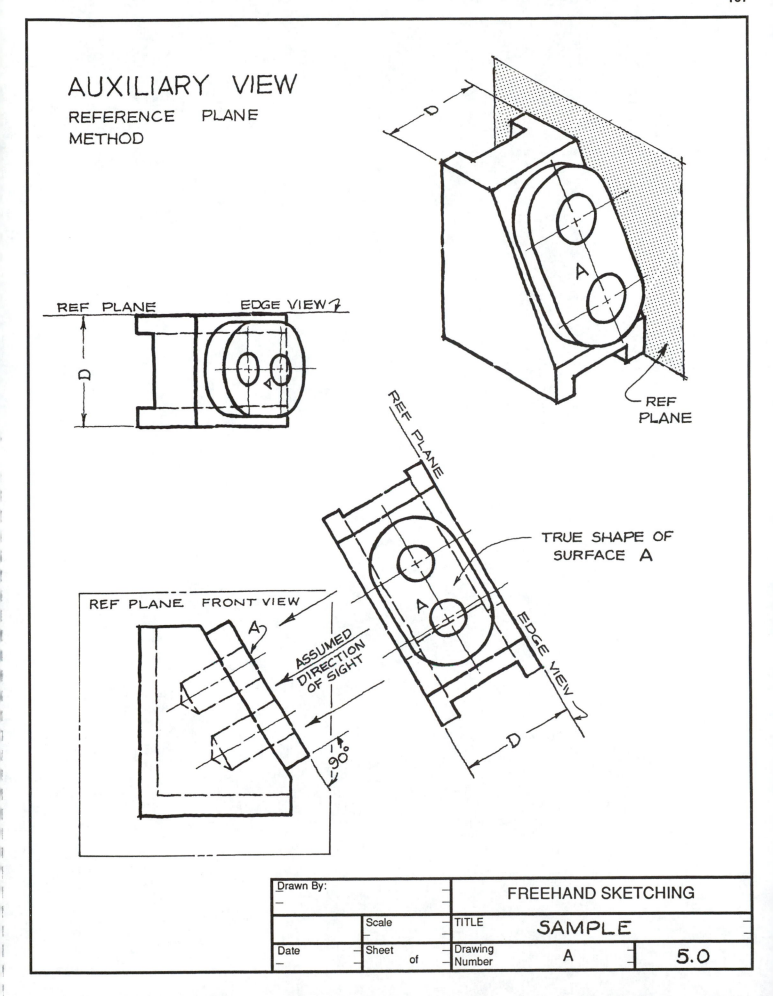

REF PLANE

EDGE VIEW

D

A

REF PLANE

TRUE SHAPE OF SURFACE A

REF PLANE   FRONT VIEW

A

ASSUMED DIRECTION OF SIGHT

90°

REF PLANE

EDGE VIEW

D

A

D

Drawn By:		FREEHAND SKETCHING	
	Scale	TITLE SAMPLE	
Date	Sheet of	Drawing Number A	5.0

A. Define the following terms.

line _____

point _____

plane _____

normal view _____

point view _____

edge view _____

reference plane _____

cutting plane _____

principal view _____

auxiliary view _____

adjacent view _____

related view _____

B. Fully label and subscript the following views.

Drawn By:		FREEHAND SKETCHING		
	Scale	TITLE AUXILIARY VIEWS		
Date	Sheet of	Drawing Number	A	5.1

CONSTRUCT A PARTIAL OR A COMPLETE AUXILIARY VIEW
OF THE OBJECTS BELOW, AS SPECIFIED.

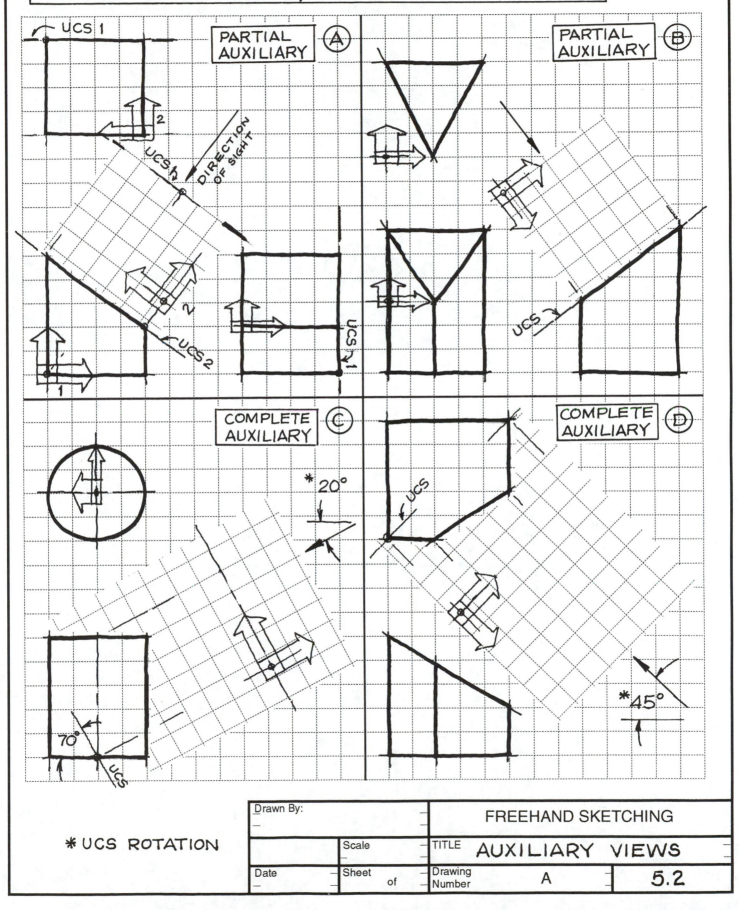

PARTIAL AUXILIARY Ⓐ

UCS 1

DIRECTION OF SIGHT

UCS 2

UCS 1

PARTIAL AUXILIARY Ⓑ

UCS

COMPLETE AUXILIARY Ⓒ

*20°

70°

UCS

COMPLETE AUXILIARY Ⓓ

UCS

*45°

* UCS ROTATION

Drawn By:		FREEHAND SKETCHING	
	Scale	TITLE AUXILIARY VIEWS	
Date	Sheet of	Drawing Number A	5.2

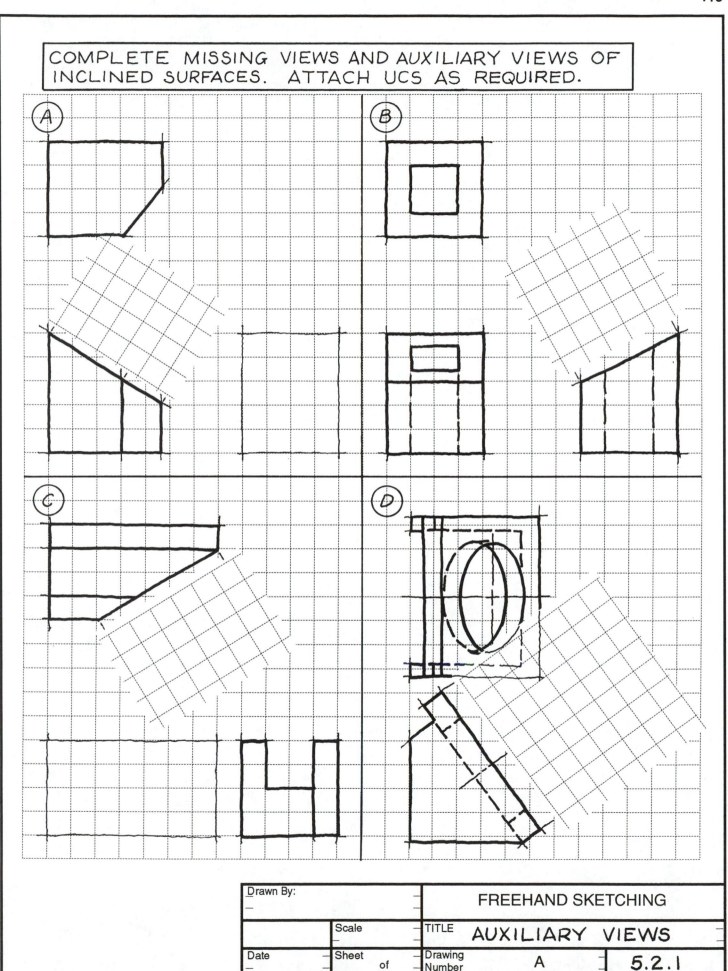

COMPLETE MISSING VIEWS AND AUXILIARY VIEWS OF INCLINED SURFACES. ATTACH UCS AS REQUIRED.

Ⓐ Ⓑ Ⓒ Ⓓ

Drawn By:			FREEHAND SKETCHING	
	Scale		TITLE AUXILIARY VIEWS	
Date	Sheet of	Drawing Number	A	5.2.1

COMPLETE A PRIMARY AUXILIARY VIEW OF THE ENTIRE OBJECT THAT INCLUDES A NORMAL VIEW OF THE TOP SURFACE.

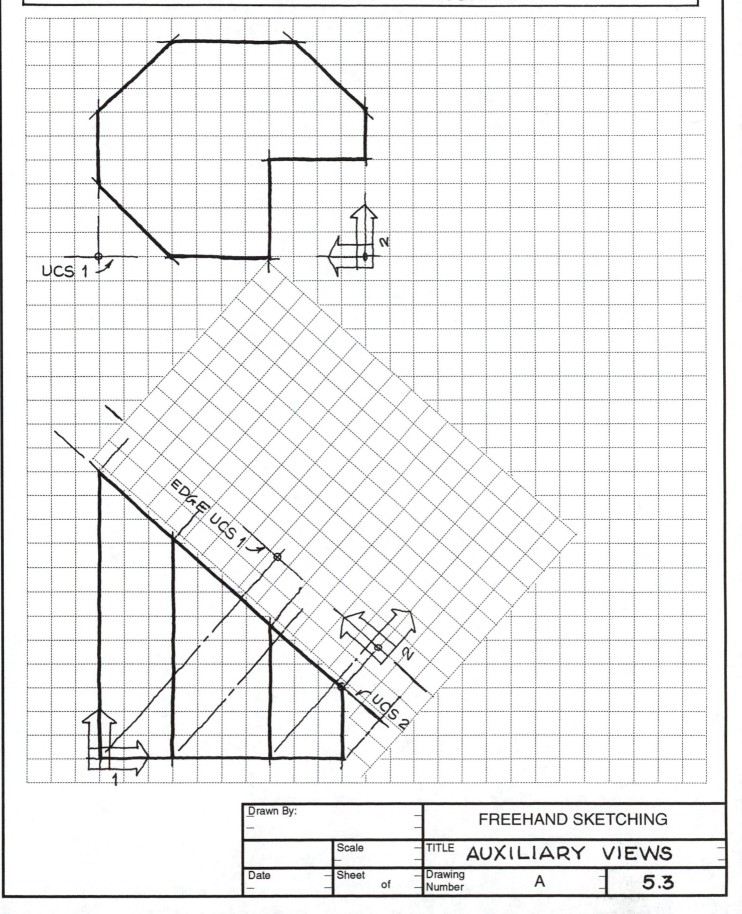

UCS 1

EDGE UCS 1

UCS 2

Drawn By:			FREEHAND SKETCHING		
	Scale		TITLE **AUXILIARY VIEWS**		
Date	Sheet	of	Drawing Number	A	**5.3**

117

COMPLETE A PRIMARY AUXILIARY VIEW OF THE ENTIRE OBJECT THAT INCLUDES A NORMAL VIEW OF THE TOP SURFACE.

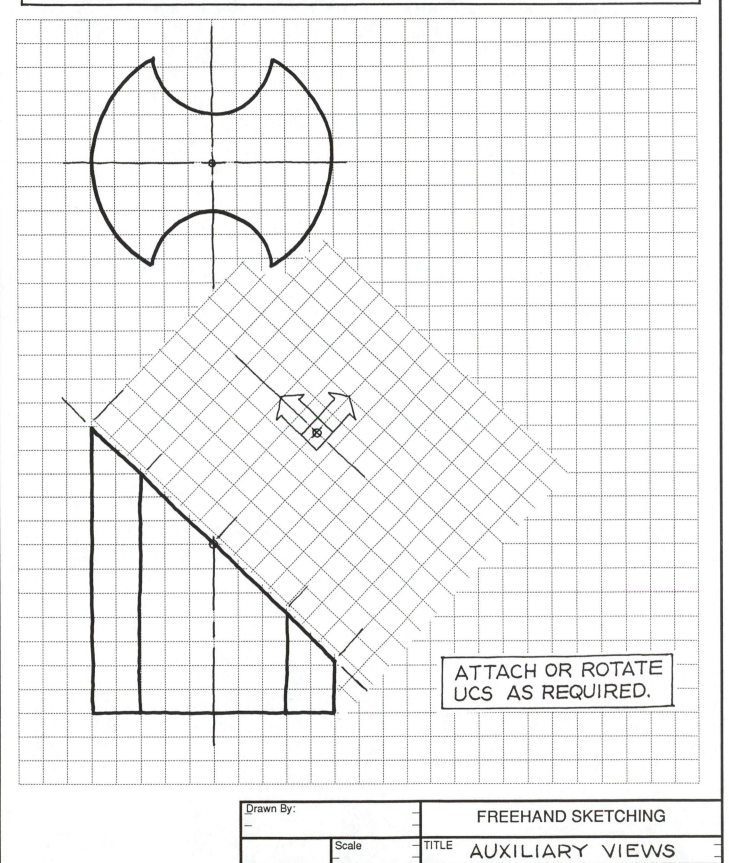

ATTACH OR ROTATE UCS AS REQUIRED.

Drawn By:		FREEHAND SKETCHING	
	Scale	TITLE AUXILIARY VIEWS	
Date	Sheet of	Drawing Number A	5.4

119

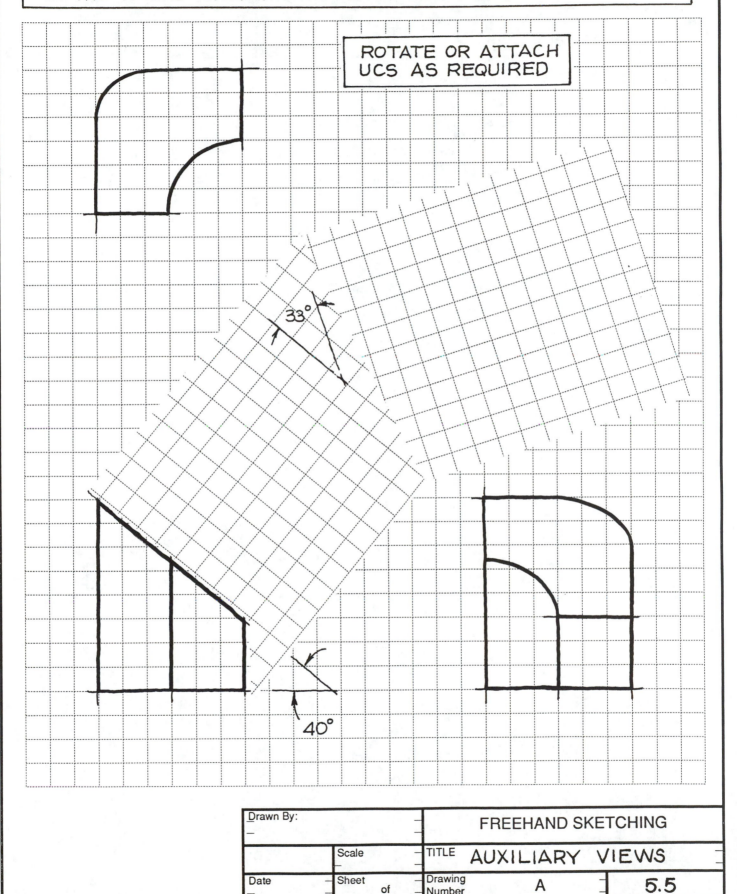

CONSTRUCT TWO COMPLETE AUXILIARY VIEWS OF THE OBJECT
IN THE AREAS SHOWN.   REFER TO SHEET 5.1.

ROTATE OR ATTACH
UCS AS REQUIRED

33°

40°

Drawn By:

FREEHAND SKETCHING

Scale | TITLE AUXILIARY VIEWS

Date | Sheet of | Drawing Number | A | 5.5

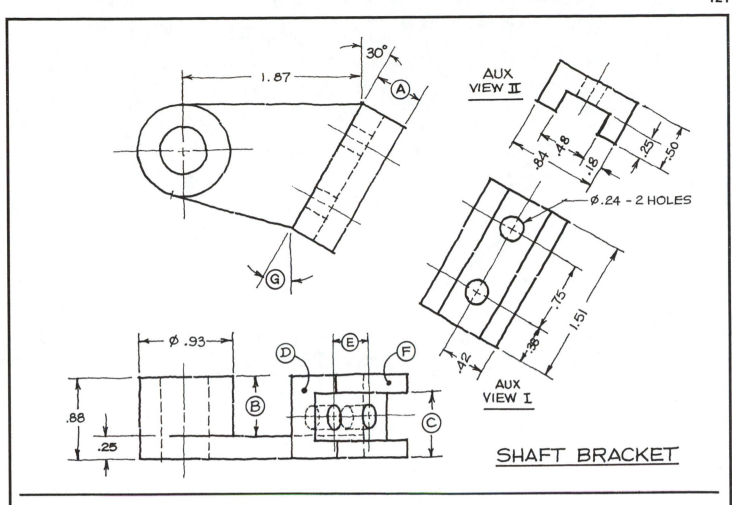

30°

1.87

(A)

(G)

AUX VIEW II

.84

.48

.18

.25

.50

Ø.24 - 2 HOLES

.75

.38

1.51

.42

AUX VIEW I

Ø .93

(D)

(E)

(F)

(B)

(C)

.88

.25

SHAFT BRACKET

QUESTIONS:

1. What is the diameter of the cylindrical end of the shaft?

2. What is dimension (A)?

3. What type of surface is (D) in the front view?

4. What is dimension (B)?

5. The actual distance between holes shown at (E) is _____ and can be accurately measured in which view?

6. Surface (F) can be seen in true shape in which view?

7. The depth of the slot is _____ and can be found in which view?

8. What is angle (G)?

ANSWERS:

1. _____

2. _____

3. _____

4. _____

5. _____

6. _____

7. _____

8. _____

Drawn By:		FREEHAND SKETCHING	
	Scale	TITLE READING DRAWINGS	
Date	Sheet of	Drawing Number A	5.6

6 Sectional Views

Sectioning — General Conditions

A sectional view is produced by passing a cutting plane through an object, taking a viewing direction normal to that plane, and removing the part of the object between the viewer and the plane. The result is a view of the object's interior detail. Objects with interior detail often require sectioning in order to allow easy visualization of cross sectional profiles. Material in contact with the cutting plane is designated by a pattern of parallel lines. Objects without interior detail do not require sectioning.

Study sheet 6.0 in detail (page 129). The location of the section is generally shown by the cutting plane-on-edge. The direction of the sectional view is generally shown by direction of sight arrows perpendicular to the cutting plane.

The cutting plane should be as straight as possible, without excessive bends and offsets. It should never double back on itself. Note the standard representation of the plane — a bold line with two dashes.

When a section appears in normal position and at the same scale as the other views, and the location of its cutting plane is unambiguous, the cutting plane may be omitted and the section not named (Fig. 6-1). However, if the location of the section is unclear, if the section has been removed from its expected position, or if the section's scale has been changed, the cutting plane should be marked (Fig. 6-2).

Assignment: Find a small object that has interior detail and can fit in the palm of your hand. Complete both an orthographic and a pictorial sketch of the object in section. Use basic proportions.

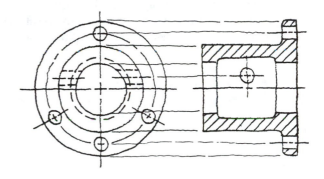

Fig. 6-1. Sectional view in principal position.

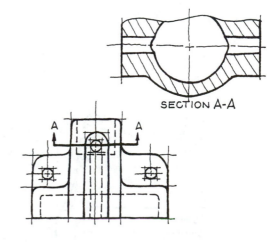

Fig. 6-2. Sectional view in removed position with change of scale.

Types of Sectional Views

When a cutting plane is passed completely through an object and divides the object equally on either side of the plane, the view is called a *full section*. Full sections are appropriate for objects whose internal features are nonsymmetrical and extend essentially from side to side (Fig. 6-3).

A *half section* is appropriate to show symmetrical detail (Fig. 6-4). It has the added advantage of being able to show the exterior in the same view as the section.

A *revolved section* (Fig. 6-5) is used to show the cross-sectional shape of a rib, spoke, or other connecting feature. The section is shown on the object, in the position where it was taken, so no cutting plane is necessary.

A *removed section* (Fig. 6-6) functions like a revolved section for objects whose profiles might be highly variable. The section is revolved but then moved off the view. This necessitates the use of a cutting plane and section name.

An *offset section* is used when features don't lie in the same plane (Fig. 6-7). Sharp edges caused by bends in the cutting plane are ignored when the section itself is drawn. The cutting plane must not bend back on itself.

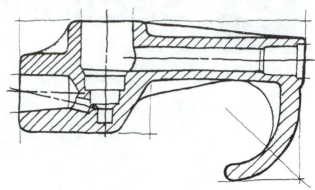

Fig.6-3. A full section.

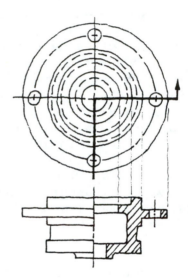

Fig.6-4. A half section.

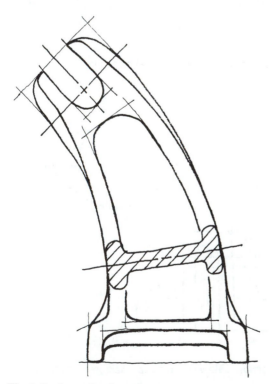

Fig.6-5. A revolved section.

Fig.6-6. A removed section.

A *broken section* is used to show interior detail at a specific location without the entire object being sectioned (Fig. 6-8).

A *sectional assembly* shows multiple parts as they are fitted together (Fig. 6-9). The rules of sectioning apply to each part separately.

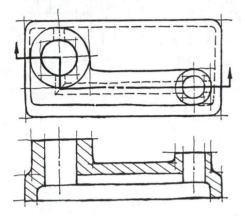

Fig. 6-7. An offset section.

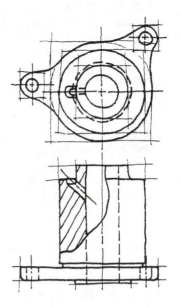

Fig. 6-8. A broken section.

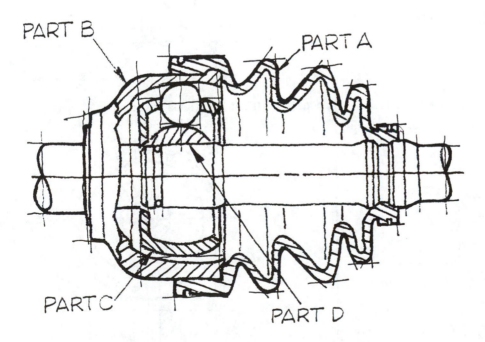

Fig. 6-9. A sectional assembly.

The Basic Rules of Sectioning

1. Don't section anything that has no interior detail. This includes rods, shafts, spheres, and other solid forms. See Fig. 6-10 (a). Use a broken section for small details on solid objects.

2. Crosshatch only material that touches the cutting plane. See Fig. 6-10 (b).

3. Revolve all radial features into the plane of the section. This includes ribs and holes shown in Fig. 6-10 (c).

4. Section features that are "full-bodied depth" or are tangent to sections that are full bodied depth. Do not section small appendages as shown in Fig. 6-10 (d).

5. Do not section ribs, spokes, or other connections. See Fig. 6-10 (e).

6. Section lines for an object are drawn the same direction anywhere that object appears on a drawing as shown in Fig. 6-10 (f). Different parts must sectioned differently.

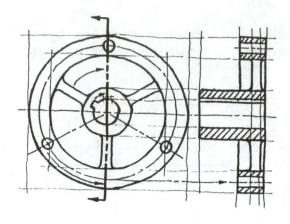

Fig. 6-10 (c). The basic rules of sectioning—revolution of radial features.

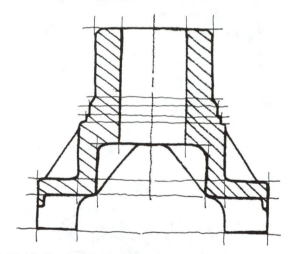

Fig. 6-10 (d). The basic rules of sectioning — sectioning features not full-bodied depth.

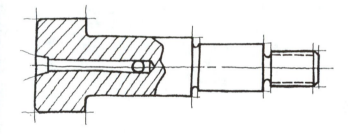

Fig. 6-10 (a). The basic rules of sectioning — interior detail.

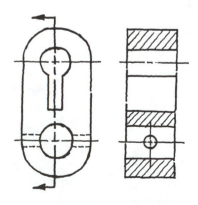

Fig. 6-10 (b). The basic rules of sectioning — cross hatching.

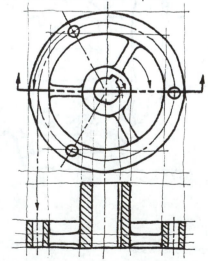

Fig. 6-10 (e). The basic rules of sectioning — ribs or spokes.

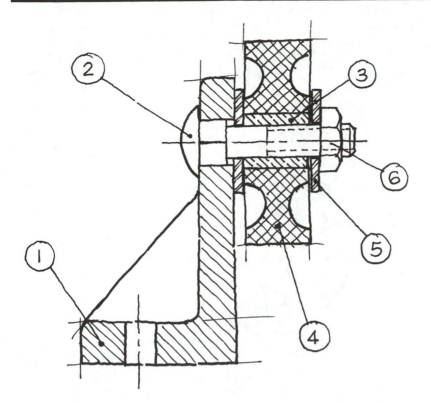

1	BASE
2	C- BOLT #
3	BUSHING #
4	ROLLER
5	WASHER (2)
6	HEX - NUT

Fig. 6-10 (f). The basic rules of sectioning — section line pattern and direction shows the same material.

CAD Example — 2D

Two-dimensional CAD uses polygon fills to show sections. Figure 6-11 shows a front view before and after sectioning operations. Note that dashed lines are changed to solid lines. These solid boundaries are then filled with a cross hatch pattern.

CAD Example — 3D

Three-dimensional CAD handles sections in different ways. In its simplist form, a wire frame model is cut by a plane (Fig. 6-12) resulting in wires that have to be joined and hatched. Solid models (Fig. 6-13) can be sectioned, resulting in a more realistic appearance. However, note in the example that the convention of revolving radial features into the plane of the section has not been followed.

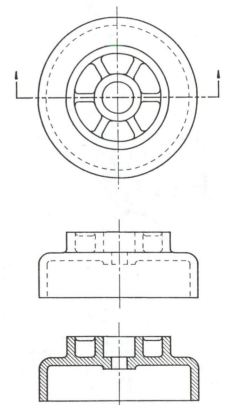

Fig. 6-11. 2D CAD sectioning.

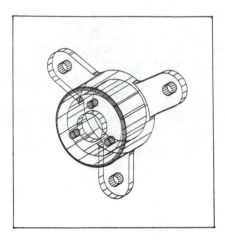 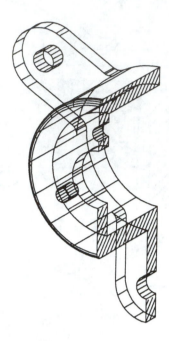

Fig. 6-11. Sectioned wireframe model.

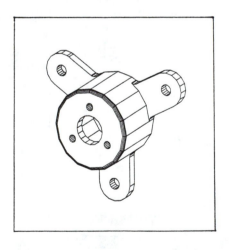 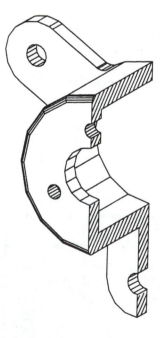

Fig. 6-12. Sectioned solid model.

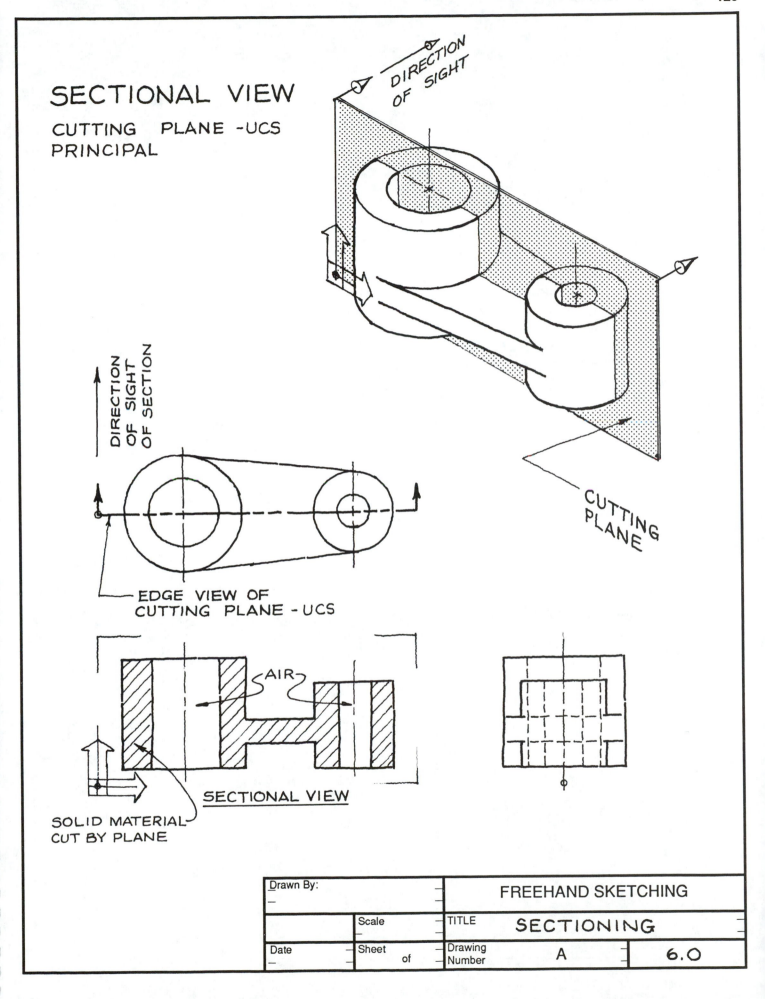

SECTIONAL VIEW
CUTTING PLANE -UCS
PRINCIPAL

DIRECTION OF SIGHT

CUTTING PLANE

DIRECTION OF SIGHT OF SECTION

EDGE VIEW OF CUTTING PLANE -UCS

AIR

SECTIONAL VIEW

SOLID MATERIAL CUT BY PLANE

Drawn By:			FREEHAND SKETCHING	
	Scale		TITLE SECTIONING	
Date	Sheet of		Drawing Number A	6.0

SKETCH THE SECTION AS CALLED FOR BY THE CUTTING PLANE.

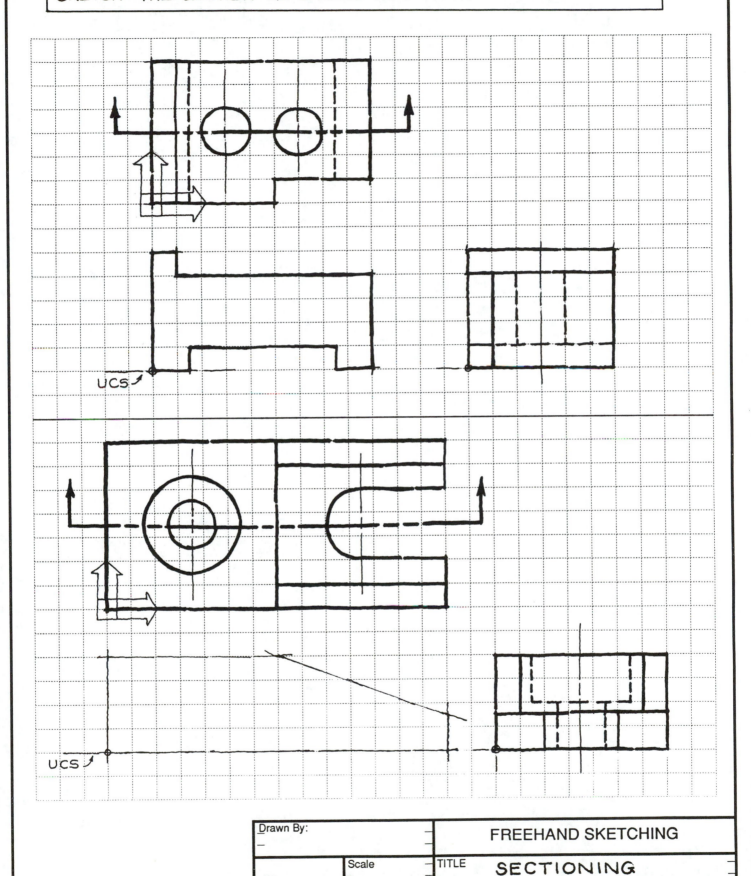

UCS

UCS

Drawn By:		FREEHAND SKETCHING		
	Scale	TITLE SECTIONING		
Date	Sheet of	Drawing Number	A	6.1

HALF-SECTION: SKETCH THE RIGHT SIDE VIEW AS CALLED FOR BY THE CUTTING PLANE. OMIT HIDDEN LINES.

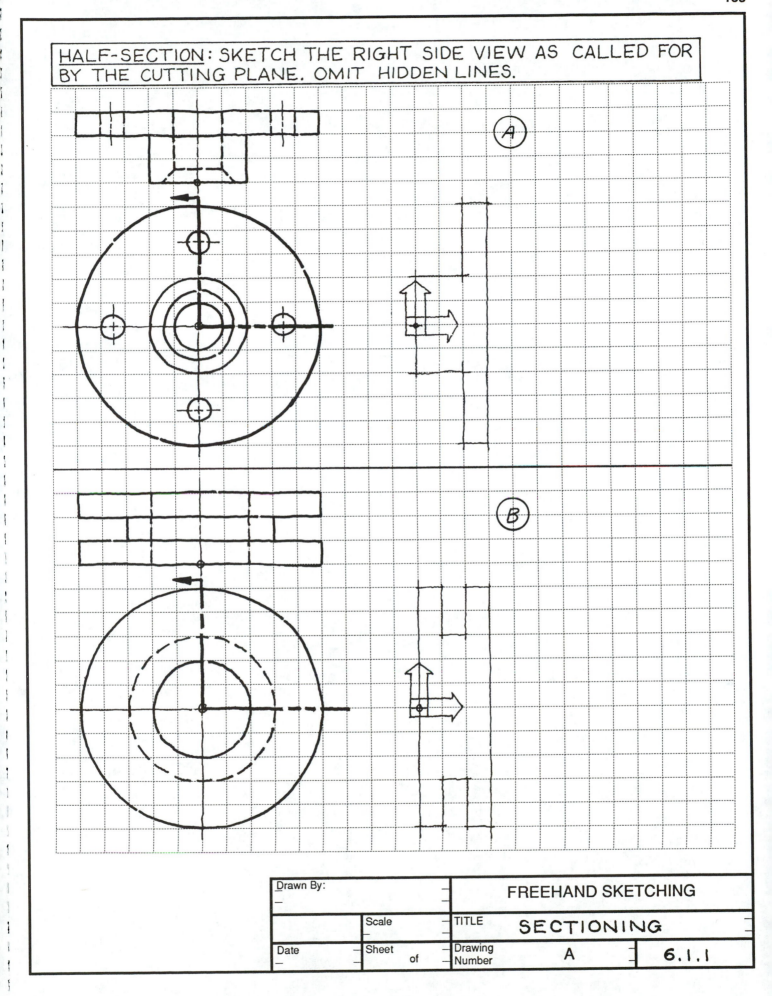

Drawn By:			FREEHAND SKETCHING	
	Scale		TITLE SECTIONING	
Date	Sheet	of	Drawing Number	A	6.1.1

ADD THE MISSING CUTTING PLANE AND COMPLETE THE
MISSING VIEW OF EACH OBJECT IN FULL SECTION

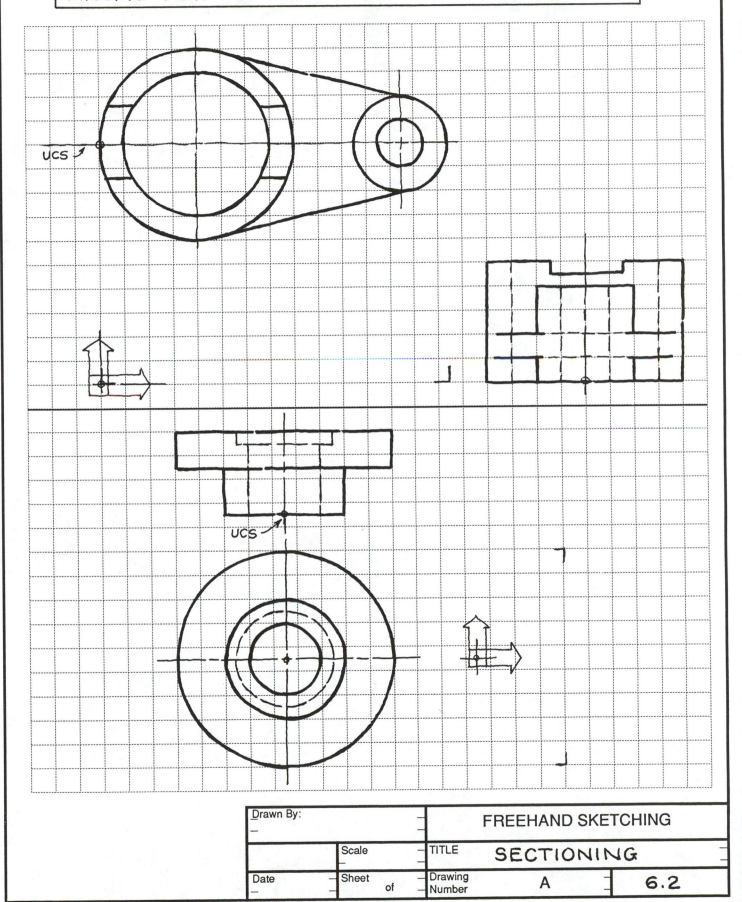

UCS

UCS

Drawn By:			FREEHAND SKETCHING		
	Scale		TITLE	SECTIONING	
Date	Sheet	of	Drawing Number	A	6.2

SKETCH THE SECTION AS CALLED FOR BY THE CUTTING PLANE.
USE STANDARD CONVENTIONS FOR REVOLVING OF RADIAL
FEATURES AND THE TREATMENT OF RIBS.

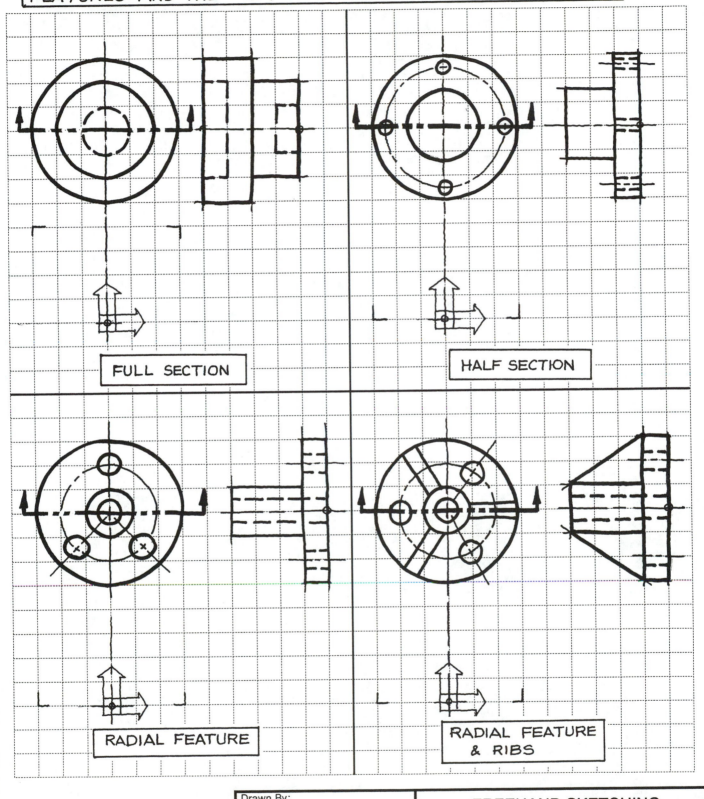

FULL SECTION

HALF SECTION

RADIAL FEATURE

RADIAL FEATURE
& RIBS

Drawn By:		FREEHAND SKETCHING		
	Scale	TITLE SECTIONING		
Date	Sheet of	Drawing Number	A	6.3

PERFORM THE SECTION. USE STANDARD TREATMENT FOR RIBS AND RADIAL FEATURES.

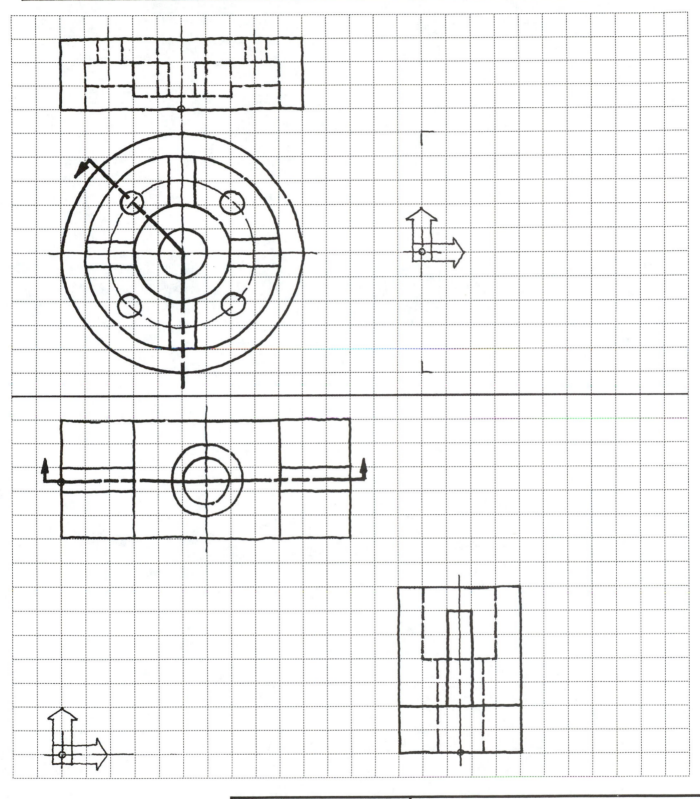

Drawn By:			FREEHAND SKETCHING	
	Scale	TITLE	SECTIONING	
Date	Sheet of	Drawing Number	A	6.3.1

141

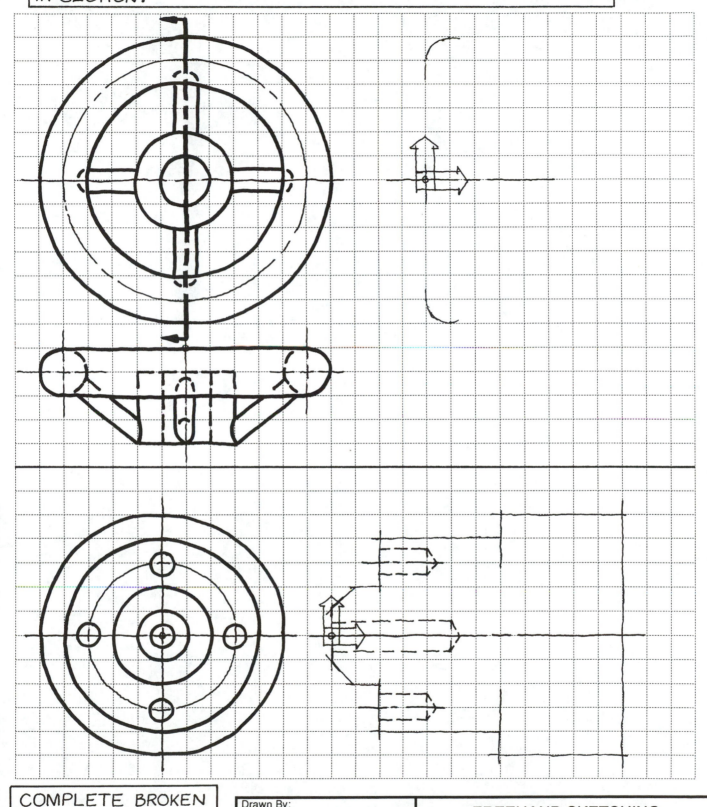

SKETCH THE SECTION AS CALLED FOR BY THE CUTTING PLANE. USE STANDARD CONVENTIONS FOR TREATMENT OF SPOKES IN SECTION.

COMPLETE BROKEN SECTIONS AS REQUIRED.

Drawn By:		FREEHAND SKETCHING	
	Scale	TITLE SECTIONING	
Date	Sheet of	Drawing Number A	6.4

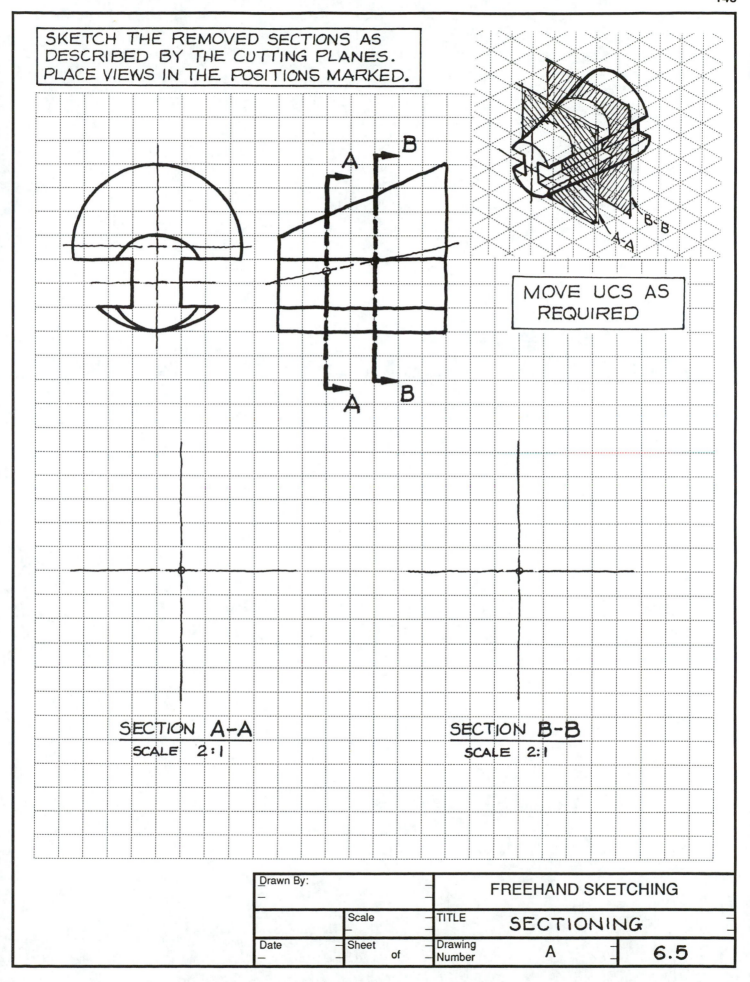

SKETCH THE REMOVED SECTIONS AS
DESCRIBED BY THE CUTTING PLANES.
PLACE VIEWS IN THE POSITIONS MARKED.

MOVE UCS AS
REQUIRED

A

B

A

B

B-B

A-A

SECTION A-A
SCALE 2:1

SECTION B-B
SCALE 2:1

Drawn By:		FREEHAND SKETCHING		
	Scale	TITLE	SECTIONING	
Date	Sheet of	Drawing Number	A	6.5

SKETCH THE REMOVED SECTIONS IN THE SPACE PROVIDED.

MOVE UCS AS
REQUIRED

A   B   C

A   B   C

SECTION A-A   SECTION B-B   SECTION C-C

Drawn By:		FREEHAND SKETCHING	
	Scale	TITLE SECTIONING	
Date	Sheet of	Drawing Number	A 6.5.1

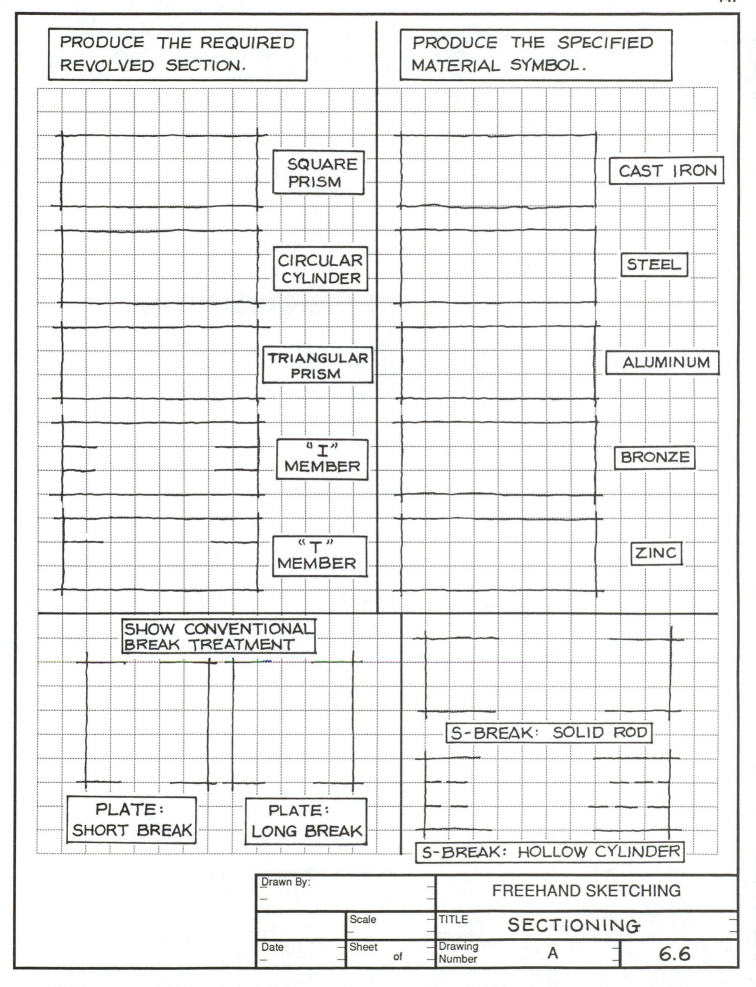

PRODUCE THE REQUIRED REVOLVED SECTION.

PRODUCE THE SPECIFIED MATERIAL SYMBOL.

SQUARE PRISM

CIRCULAR CYLINDER

TRIANGULAR PRISM

"I" MEMBER

"T" MEMBER

CAST IRON

STEEL

ALUMINUM

BRONZE

ZINC

SHOW CONVENTIONAL BREAK TREATMENT

PLATE: SHORT BREAK

PLATE: LONG BREAK

S-BREAK: SOLID ROD

S-BREAK: HOLLOW CYLINDER

Drawn By:		FREEHAND SKETCHING	
	Scale	TITLE SECTIONING	
Date	Sheet of	Drawing Number A	6.6

IN EACH PROBLEM, DETERMINE THE CORRECT TREATMENT FOR THE SECTIONED FEATURES.

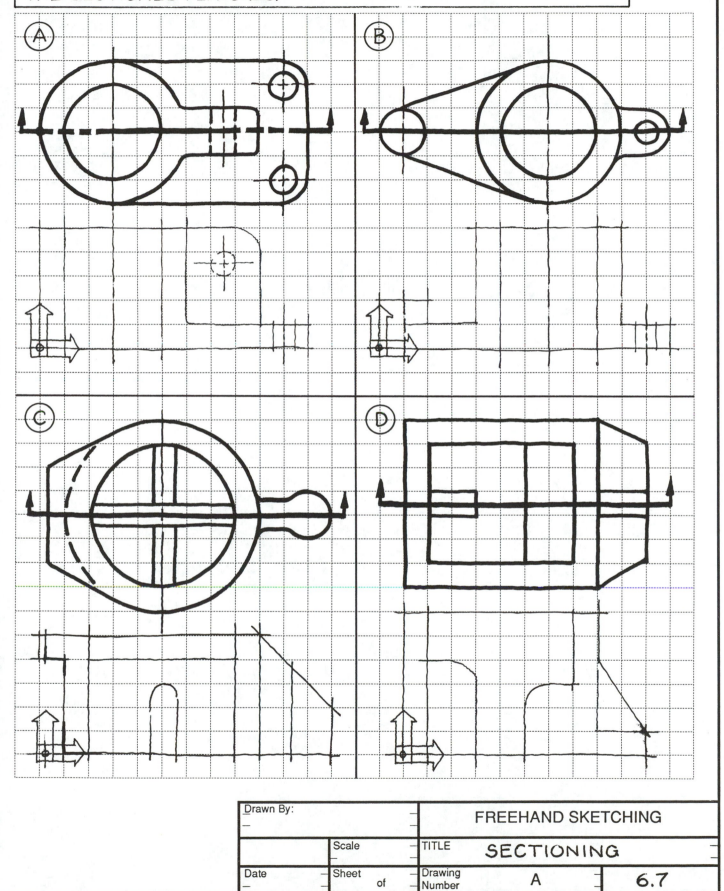

Drawn By:			FREEHAND SKETCHING	
	Scale		TITLE SECTIONING	
Date	Sheet	of	Drawing Number A	6.7

151

SHOW POSITION OF OFFSET CUTTING PLANE IN PROBLEMS A & B.
COMPLETE FRONT VIEW IN PROBLEM C AS A FULL OFFSET SECTION.

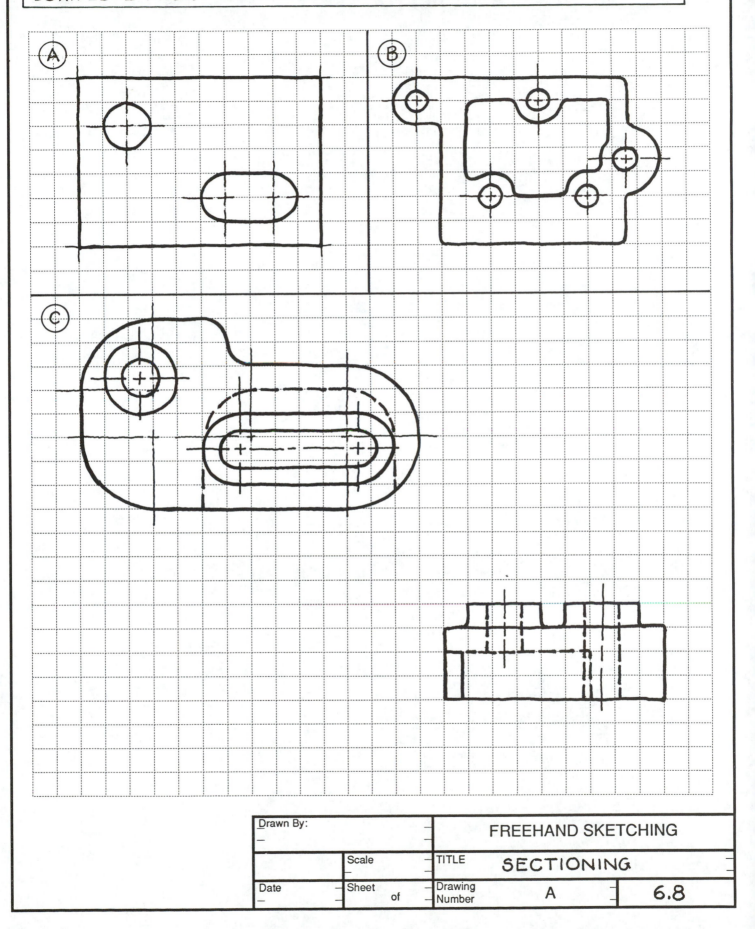

Drawn By:		FREEHAND SKETCHING		
	Scale	TITLE	SECTIONING	
Date	Sheet of	Drawing Number	A	6.8

153

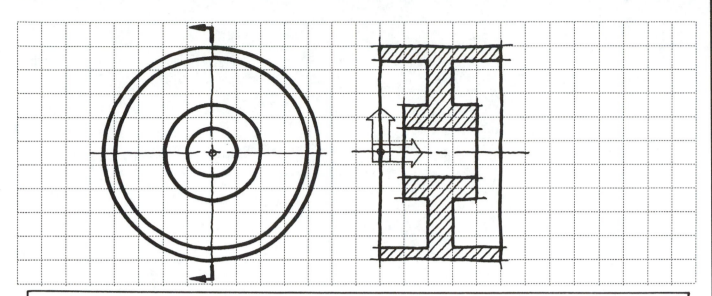

GIVEN: FRONT AND RIGHT SIDE (FULL SECTION) VIEWS OF A GEAR BLANK.
COMPLETE AN ISOMETRIC SKETCH IN HALF-SECTION.

Drawn By:			FREEHAND SKETCHING	
	Scale		TITLE SECTIONING	
Date	Sheet of		Drawing Number	A	6.9

SHOW THE INCOMPLETE VIEW AS A SECTIONAL ASSEMBLY.

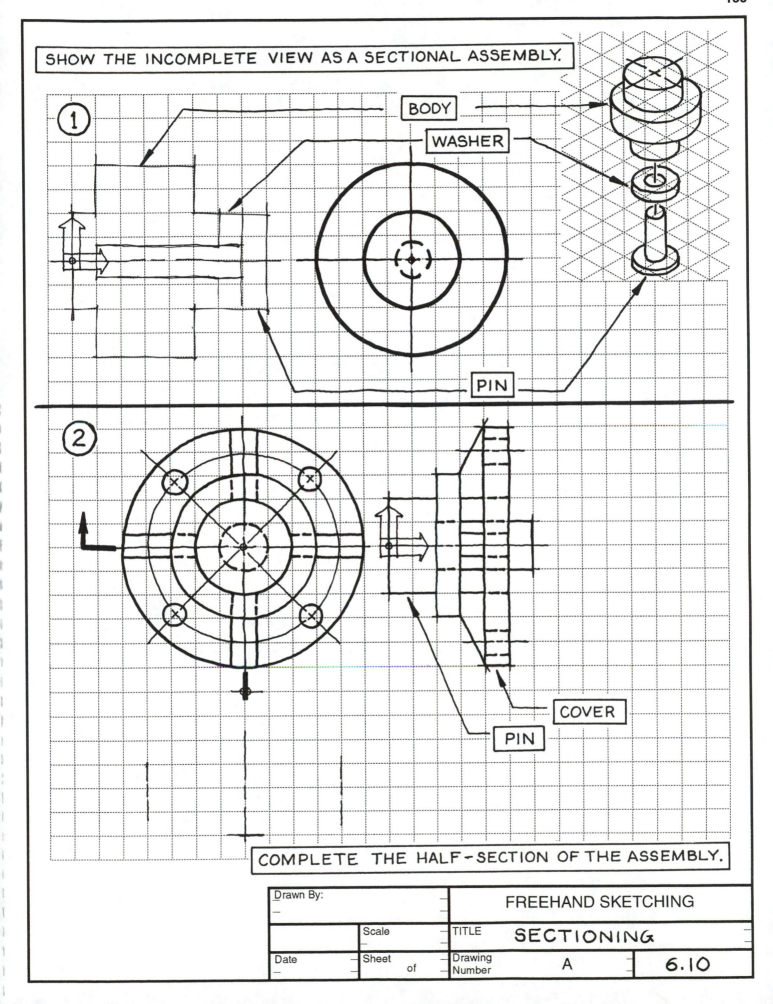

① BODY
WASHER
PIN

② COMPLETE THE HALF-SECTION OF THE ASSEMBLY.
COVER
PIN

Drawn By:			FREEHAND SKETCHING		
	Scale		TITLE SECTIONING		
Date	Sheet of		Drawing Number	A	6.10

THE FULL-SIZE DETAILS PRESENTED ON THIS PAGE ARE TO BE USED
TO COMPLETE THE SECTIONAL ASSEMBLY ON SHEET 5.12

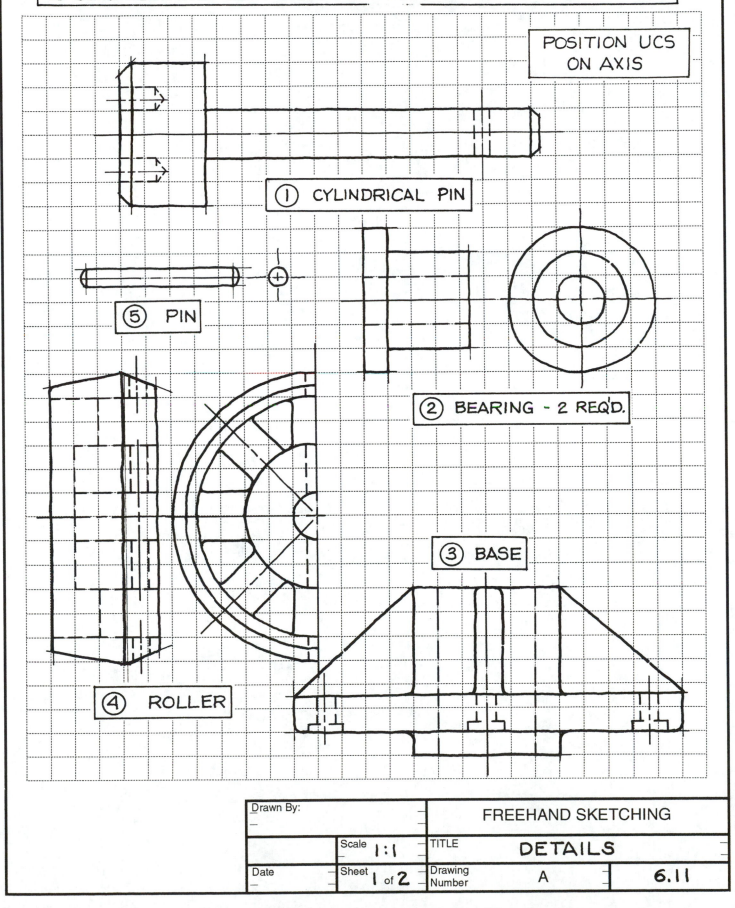

POSITION UCS
ON AXIS

① CYLINDRICAL PIN

⑤ PIN

② BEARING - 2 REQ'D.

③ BASE

④ ROLLER

Drawn By:		FREEHAND SKETCHING		
	Scale 1:1	TITLE	DETAILS	
Date	Sheet 1 of 2	Drawing Number	A	6.11

USING THE DETAILS ON SHEET 6.11, COMPLETE A FULL SECTIONAL
ASSEMBLY DRAWING IN THE SPACE PROVIDED. NOTE THAT THE
PARTS HAVE BEEN IDENTIFIED.

POSITION UCS
ON AXIS

Drawn By:		FREEHAND SKETCHING	
	Scale 1:1	TITLE ASSEMBLY	
Date	Sheet 2 of 2	Drawing Number A	6.12

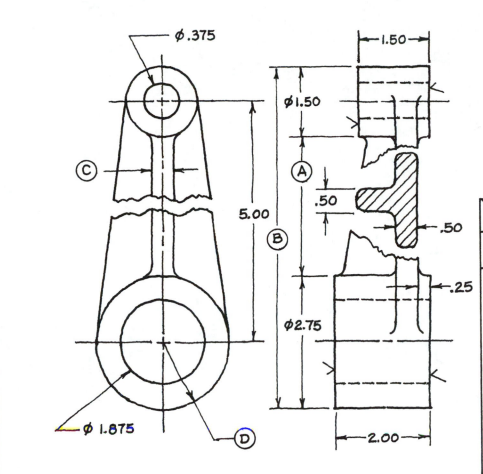

φ.375

1.50

φ1.50

Ⓒ

Ⓐ

.50

5.00

Ⓑ

.50

.50

.25

φ2.75

φ 1.875

Ⓓ

2.00

SHAFT HANGER

MATL – CI, 4 REQD

NOTE: UNLESS OTHERWISE
SPECIFIED –
ROUNDS AND FILLETS .08R
TOLERANCE ON TWO-DECIMAL
DIMENSIONS ±.02
TOLERANCE ON THREE-DECIMAL
DIMENSIONS ±.004

QUESTIONS:

ANSWERS:

1. How many surfaces on the casting require finishing?

1. _____

2. What type of section is used?

2. _____

3. What is the minimum allowable center-to-center distance between holes?

3. _____

4. What is the maximum allowable height of the part at Ⓑ ?

4. _____

5. What are the maximum and minimum allowable dimensions for Ⓐ and Ⓒ?

5. _____

6. What type of break line is used on the sectional view?

6. _____

7. What is the maximum permissable wall thickness at the large hole?

7. _____

8. What are the nominal dimensions for Ⓐ , Ⓑ , Ⓒ , and Ⓓ?

8. _____

Drawn By:		FREEHAND SKETCHING	
	Scale **2:1**	TITLE **READING DRAWINGS**	
Date	Sheet of	Drawing Number A	**6.13**

Dimensioning Practices

Dimensioning — General Conditions

The full description of an object includes its shape, its size, and any and all information necessary for it to be manufactured. In previous chapters you gained experience in describing the appearance of an object. In this chapter you will learn the basics of describing its size.

Most sketches are made *not to scale* (NTS). This means that the appearance is proportional at best. The numbers associated with the sketch represent actual sizes. This is shown in Fig. 7-1. Because sketches are approximations, correct dimensions are very important.

A dimension is recorded according to a set of specific rules. In its most basic form a dimension has two components:

1. the numerical size (size dimension), and

2. the position of the dimension (location dimension).

A correctly dimensioned drawing contains size and location information necessary and sufficient for it to be produced within an acceptable range of variability. Figure 7-2 shows the necessary and sufficient information to locate and size a hole on a plate.

Dimension Symbology

Dimensions can be linear, radial, angular, or for diameters. Figure 7-3 shows the components of these basic dimension types. Also standard industrial practice is to use a textual note whenever possible.

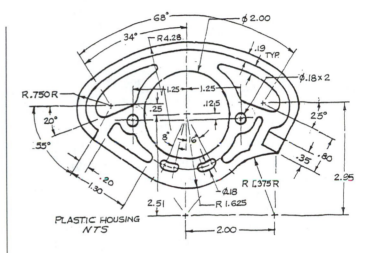

Fig. 7-1. A proportional sketch with dimensional information.

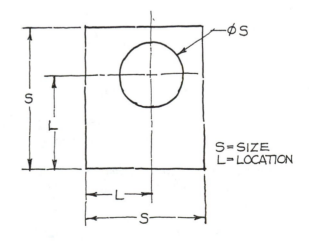

Fig. 7-2. Size and location dimensions.

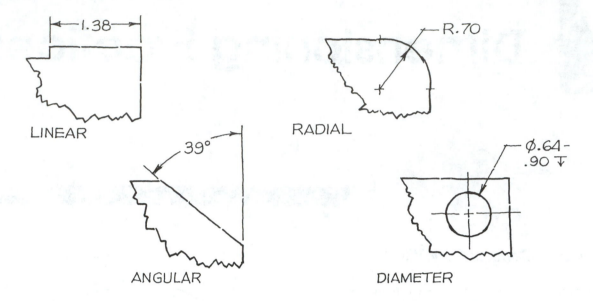

Fig. 7-3. Dimension symbology.

Sheet 7.0 (page 167) outlines the steps you should follow in dimensioning an object. Spend some time with this sheet before you start on the exercises. Note in Step 2 that holes are dimensioned by their diameter and that curved corners are dimensioned by their radii. Step 4 shows that a dimension can function both as location and size. Step 6 shows a general note. Also, in this final step dimensions, called datums, are grouped from common base lines.

Dimensioning Geometric Primitives

All parts, no matter how sophisticated, can be broken down into primitives shapes. Correct dimensioning practice is then a process of correctly sizing and locating features within the overall structure of an object. Figure 7-4 depicts the necessary size information for several primitive shapes. Keep two points in mind:

1. Holes are dimensioned in the view in which the axis of the hole appears as a point (circle view of hole).

2. Cylinder diameters are dimensioned in the view in which the axis of the cylinder appears normally (rectangular view of cylinder).

Figure 7-5 applies these techniques to composite geometry.

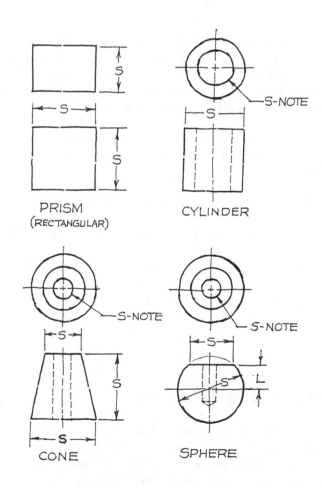

Fig. 7-4. Dimensions of primitives.

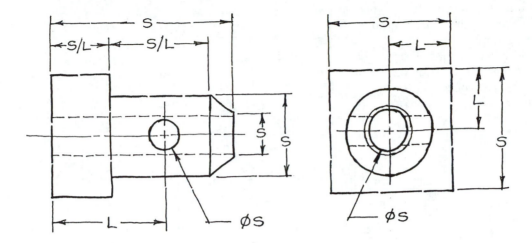

Fig. 7-5. A dimensioned composite object.

Technical Lettering

In a dimensioned sketch, legible lettering is of paramount importance. Never letter without using light guide lines. You should have been using the small tick marks in the lab sheet title blocks to position guidelines. Figure 7-6 shows appropriate technical lettering.

Assignment: Complete a technical sketch of an object you can easily hold in your hand. Use ortho grid paper. Using dimensioning techniques shown in Figs. 7-3 and 7-4, show overall height, width, and depth.

Notes

Many times writing a textual note is clearer than inserting traditional dimensions. Figure 7-7 shows a hole detail. The required size information has been recorded both in dimension and note form. Which do you think is more efficient?

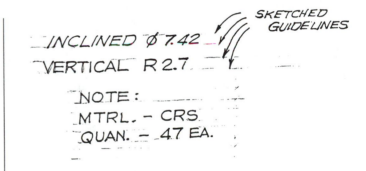

Fig. 7-6. Technical lettering.

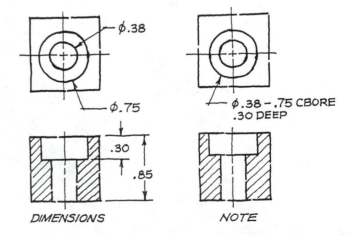

Fig. 7-7. Comparison of dimensions and notes.

CAD Example — 2D

CAD drafting programs include semiautomatic dimensioning functions. This means that the program provides for all sizes; you must determine which dimensions are necessary and where to place them. Two-dimensional CAD automates the drawing of extension and dimension lines, arrowheads, and dimension text. CAD dimensions are consistent and readable.

CAD Example — 3D

Three-dimensional CAD models do not normally need to be dimensioned. The numerical information associated with the model can be interpreted directly by numerically controlled machine tools and processing equipment. If the geometric data need to be communicated to a human machine operator or technician, the model itself can be dimensioned (Fig. 7-8) or the model can be *smashed* into 2D views and dimensioned traditionally (Fig. 7-9).

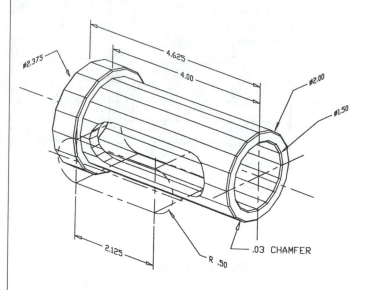

Fig. 7-8. An edited dimensioned model.

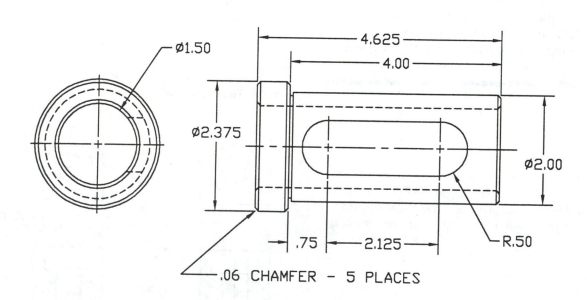

Fig. 7-9. Model smashed and dimensioned.

FUNDAMENTALS OF DIMENSIONING

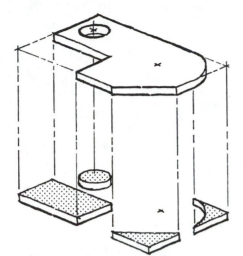

1 DIVIDE OBJECT INTO COMPONENT GEOMETRIC SHAPES.

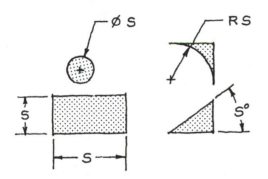

2 DETERMINE SIZE DIMENSIONS FOR EACH COMPONENT SHAPE.

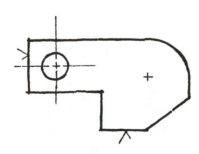

3 IDENTIFY LOCATING CENTER LINES AND FINISHED SURFACES.

* ALSO SIZE DIMENSIONS

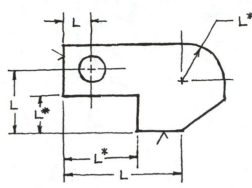

4 DETERMINE LOCATION DIMENSIONS FOR EACH COMPONENT SHAPE.

D = .125 PLATE

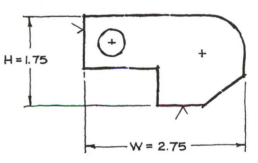

H = 1.75
W = 2.75

5 SHOW OVERALL DIMENSIONS OF HEIGHT, WIDTH, AND DEPTH.

MTRL: .125 ALUM PL
TOLER.: +/- .01
QUAN. : 1700
PART No. NF89

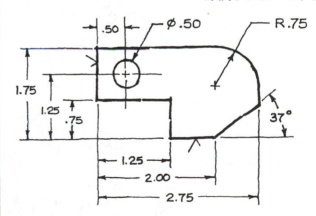

6 ADD REQUIRED NOTES OR PROCEDURES.

Drawn By:		FREEHAND SKETCHING	
	Scale NTS	TITLE INFORMATION SHEET	
Date	Sheet of	Drawing Number	A	7.0

GIVEN AN OBJECT AND EXTENSION LINES, ADD DIMENSION LINES AND TERMINATORS.

PLACE THE NUMERICAL VALUE 4.56 ON A COMPLETE DIMENSION.

DIMENSION THE .75 RADIUS ROUNDED CORNER AND .25 DIAMETER HOLE.

DIMENSION THE 3.5 DIAMETER CYLINDER AND .50 DIAMETER HOLE.

Drawn By:		FREEHAND SKETCHING	
	Scale N/A	TITLE DIMENSIONING	
Date	Sheet of	Drawing Number A	7.1

PIPE DATA: 1.50 O.D. / 1.00 I.D. / 2.25 LONG. USE UNIDIRECTIONAL DIMENSIONING METHOD.

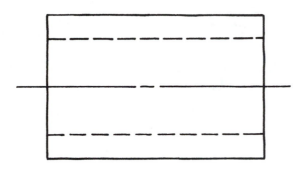
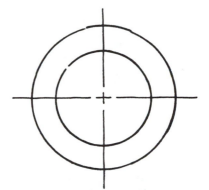

DIMENSION THE CYLINDRICAL PLUG USING COMMON FRACTIONS. USE THE ALIGNED METHOD.

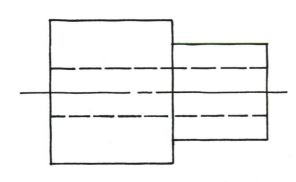
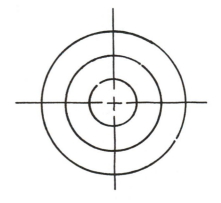

Drawn By:		FREEHAND SKETCHING	
	Scale N/A	TITLE DIMENSIONING	
Date	Sheet of	Drawing Number A	7.1.1

PLACE DIMENSIONS ON ROUNDED CORNERS AND HOLES.

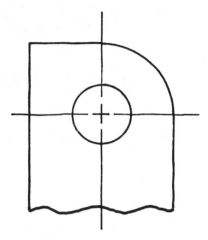

$\frac{3}{4}$ ROUNDED CORNER WITH $\frac{5}{16}$ φ HOLE.

PLACE DIMENSIONS ON ROUNDED CORNERS AND HOLES.

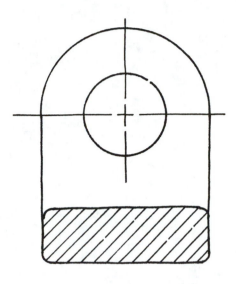

.875 φ ROUNDED END WITH A .875 φ HOLE.

PLACE DIMENSIONS ON ANGLED CORNERS.

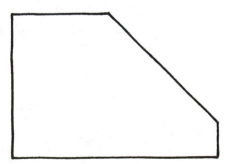

$1\frac{1}{8}$ X 45° ANGLED CORNER BY ANGULAR MEASUREMENT.

PLACE DIMENSIONS ON ANGLED CORNERS.

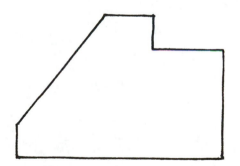

.750 X 1.125 ANGLED CORNER BY LINEAR COORDINATES.

Drawn By:		FREEHAND SKETCHING		
	Scale N/A	TITLE DIMENSIONING		
Date	Sheet of	Drawing Number	A	7.1.2

COMPLETE SIZE (S) AND LOCATION (L) DIMENSIONS. USE (S) AND (L) RATHER THAN NUMERICAL VALUES.

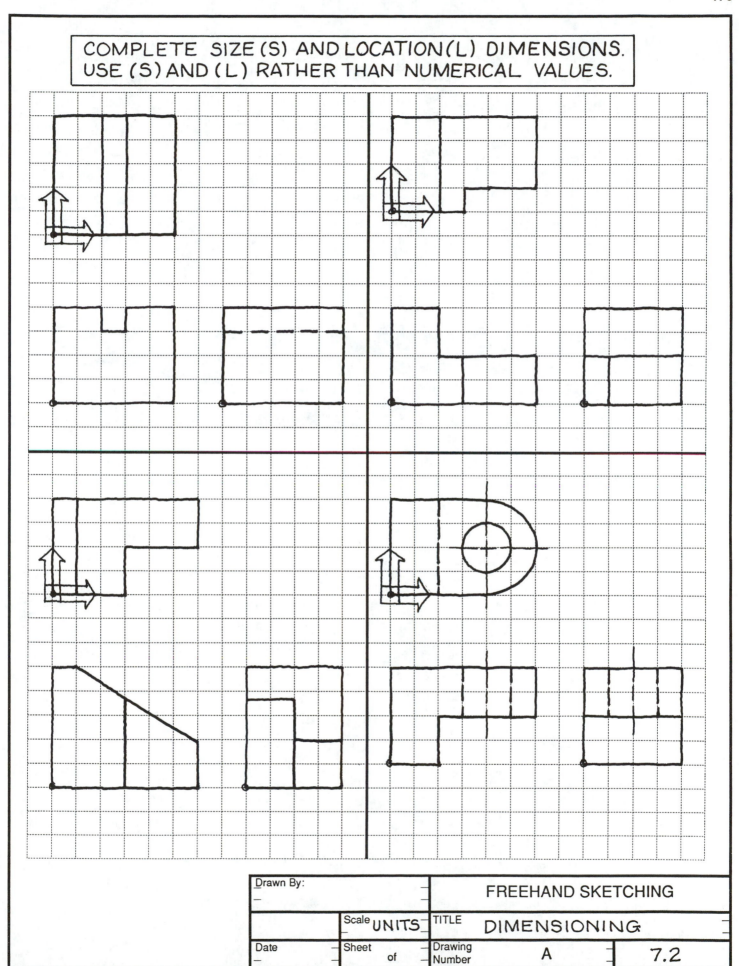

Drawn By:			FREEHAND SKETCHING		
	Scale UNITS	TITLE	DIMENSIONING		
Date	Sheet of	Drawing Number	A		7.2

177

PROBLEM A: UNIDIRECTIONAL TO TWO DECIMAL PLACES.
PROBLEM B: ALIGNED - TWO DECIMAL PLACES.

A

U.CS

B

U.CS

NOTE: .25 GRID

Drawn By:		FREEHAND SKETCHING	
	Scale NOTED	TITLE DIMENSIONING	
Date	Sheet of	Drawing Number	A	7.2.1

COMPLETE SIZE (S) AND LOCATION (L) DIMENSIONS.
USE (S) AND (L) RATHER THAN NUMERICAL VALUES.

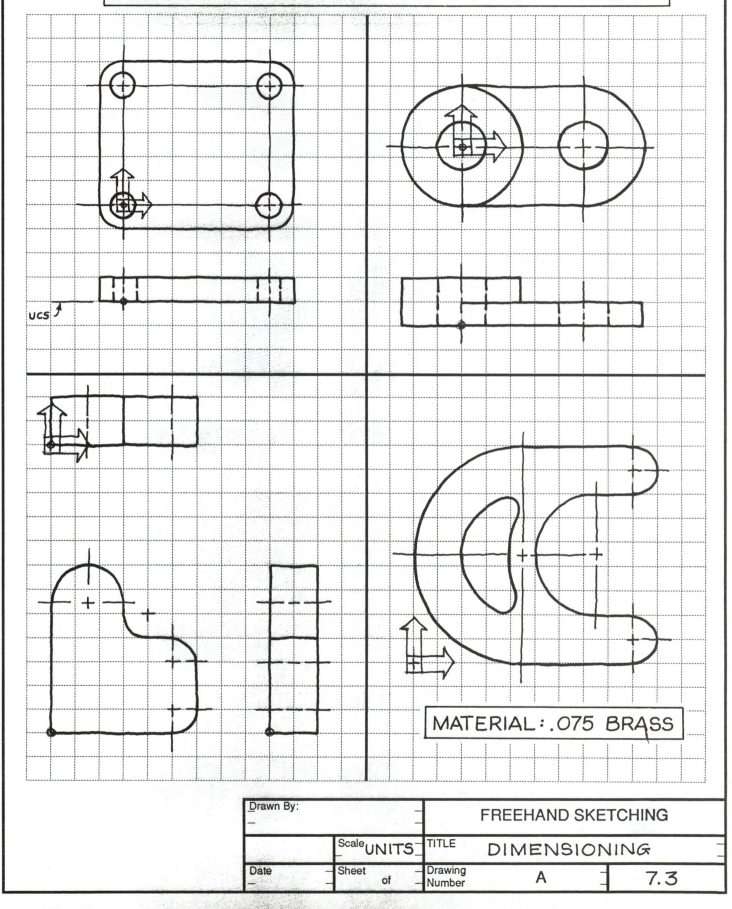

UCS

MATERIAL:.075 BRASS

Drawn By:			FREEHAND SKETCHING		
	Scale	UNITS	TITLE	DIMENSIONING	
Date	Sheet	of	Drawing Number	A	7.3

PROBLEM A: ADD REQUIRED NOTES & DIMENSIONS. GRID IS .25".
PROBLEM B: ADD REQUIRED NOTES & DIMENSIONS. GRID IS .125."

Ⓐ

Ⓑ

NOTE: BOTH DONE
TO TWO DECIMAL
PLACES.

Drawn By:		FREEHAND SKETCHING	
Scale NOTED	TITLE	DIMENSIONING	
Date	Sheet of	Drawing Number	A	7.3.1

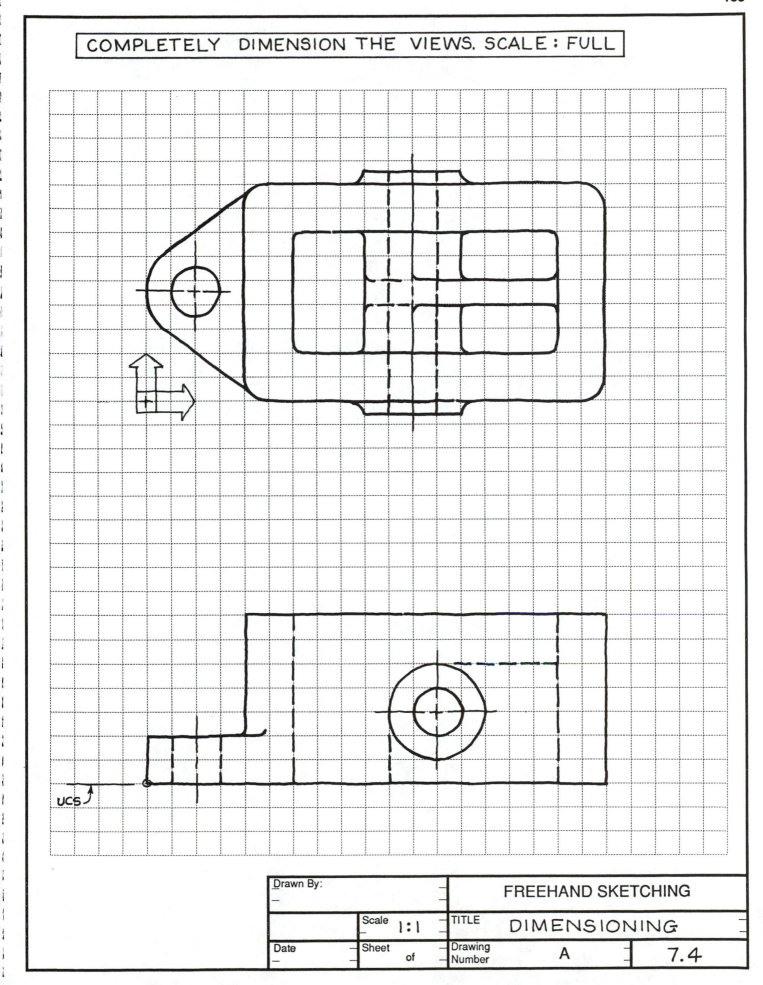

COMPLETELY DIMENSION THE VIEWS. SCALE: FULL

UCS

Drawn By:			FREEHAND SKETCHING	
	Scale 1:1	TITLE	DIMENSIONING	
Date	Sheet of	Drawing Number	A	7.4

PROBLEM A: NOTES & DIMENSIONS TO TWO DECIMAL PLACES. GRID=.125."
PROBLEM B: NOTES & DIMENSIONS TO TWO DECIMAL PLACES. GRID=.25."

Ⓐ

Ⓑ

Drawn By:		FREEHAND SKETCHING		
	Scale NOTED	TITLE DIMENSIONING		
Date	Sheet of	Drawing Number	A	7.4.1

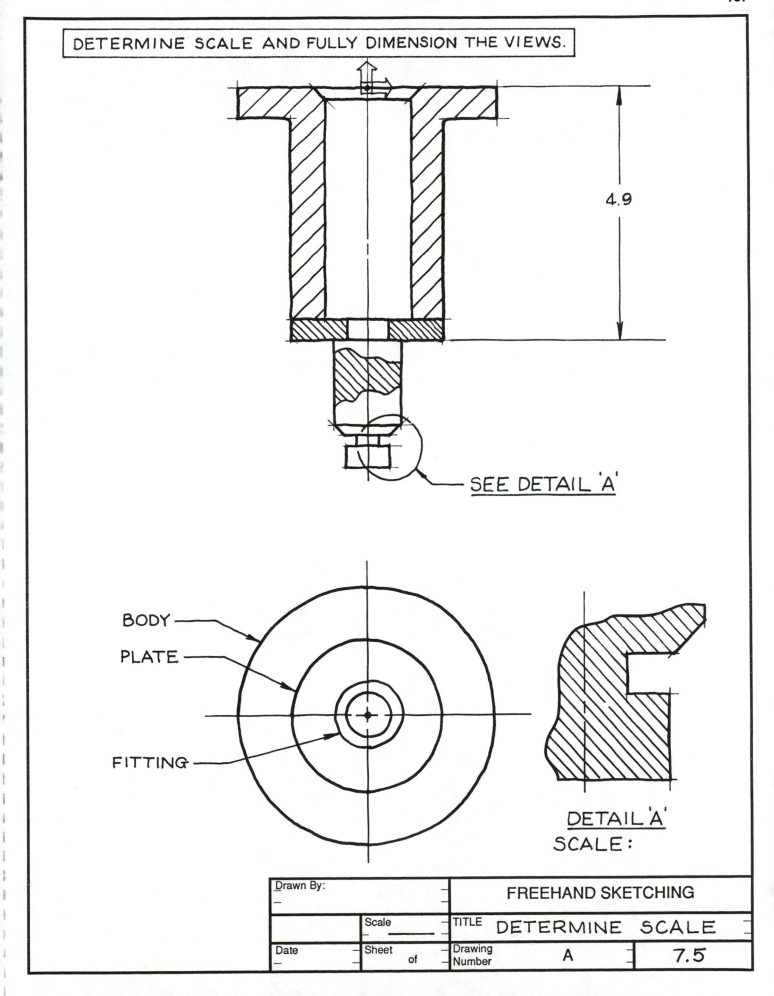

DETERMINE SCALE AND FULLY DIMENSION THE VIEWS.

4.9

SEE DETAIL 'A'

BODY

PLATE

FITTING

DETAIL 'A'
SCALE:

Drawn By:		FREEHAND SKETCHING	
	Scale ____	TITLE DETERMINE SCALE	
Date	Sheet of	Drawing Number A	7.5

DEVELOP A SCALE FOR THIS SECTIONAL VIEW.
RECORD DIMENSIONS IN TABULAR FORM.

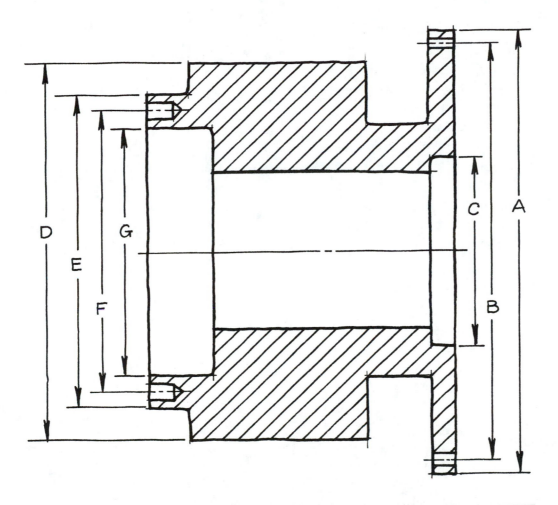

TABULAR DIMENSIONS						
A	B	C	D	E	F	G
8.6						

Drawn By:		FREEHAND SKETCHING	
	Scale 1:1	TITLE DIMENSIONING	
Date	Sheet of	Drawing Number	A	7.6

RECORD VALUES IN <u>DATUM</u> DIMENSIONING FORMAT.

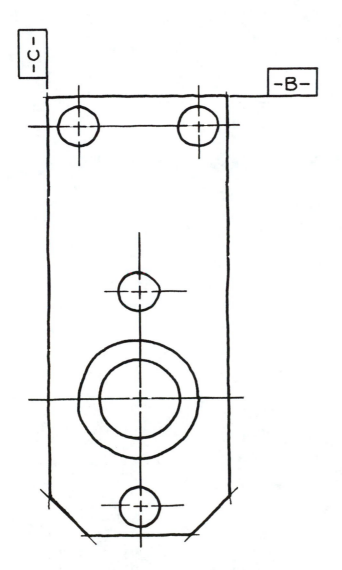

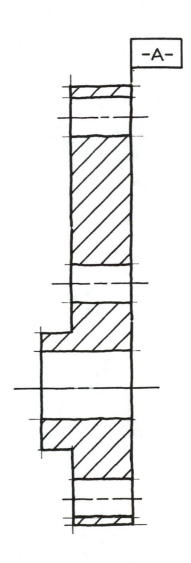

<u>TERMINAL TOP</u>

Drawn By:		FREEHAND SKETCHING	
	Scale 1:1	TITLE DIMENSIONING	
Date	Sheet of	Drawing Number A	7.7

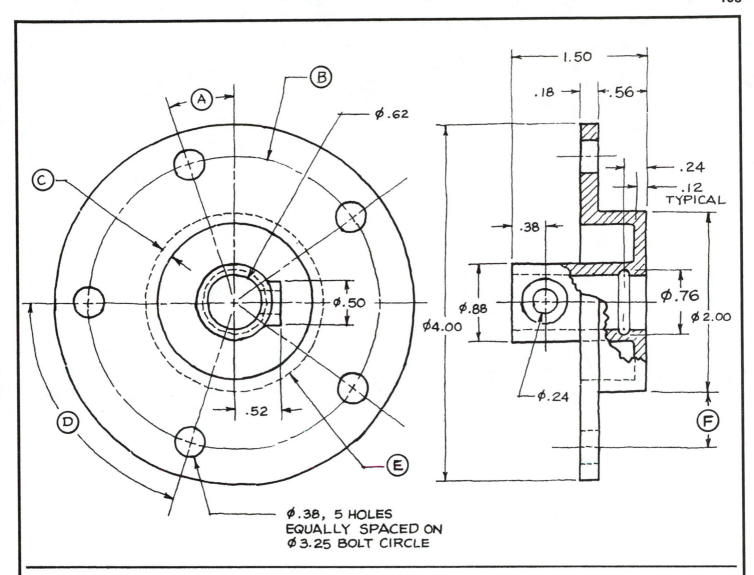

Ø.62

Ø.50

.52

Ø4.00

Ø.88

1.50

.18

.56

.38

.24

.12 TYPICAL

Ø.76

Ø2.00

Ø.24

Ø.38, 5 HOLES
EQUALLY SPACED ON
Ø3.25 BOLT CIRCLE

QUESTIONS:

1. What type of sectional view is shown?
2. What is angle (A)?
3. What is the thickness at (C)?
4. How thick is the largest flange?
5. What is diameter (B)?
6. What is angle (D)?
7. What is diameter (E)?
8. What is dimension (F)?

ANSWERS:

1. _____
2. _____
3. _____
4. _____
5. _____
6. _____
7. _____
8. _____

Drawn By:			FREEHAND SKETCHING	
	Scale NTS	TITLE	READING EXERCISE	
Date	Sheet of	Drawing Number	A	7.8

Drawn By:				FREEHAND SKETCHING	
	Scale		TITLE	PLAIN SHEET	
Date	Sheet	of	Drawing Number	A	

Drawn By:			FREEHAND SKETCHING		
	Scale		TITLE	PLAIN SHEET	
Date	Sheet	of	Drawing Number	A	

Drawn By:			FREEHAND SKETCHING		
	Scale		TITLE	PLAIN SHEET	
Date	Sheet	of	Drawing Number	A	

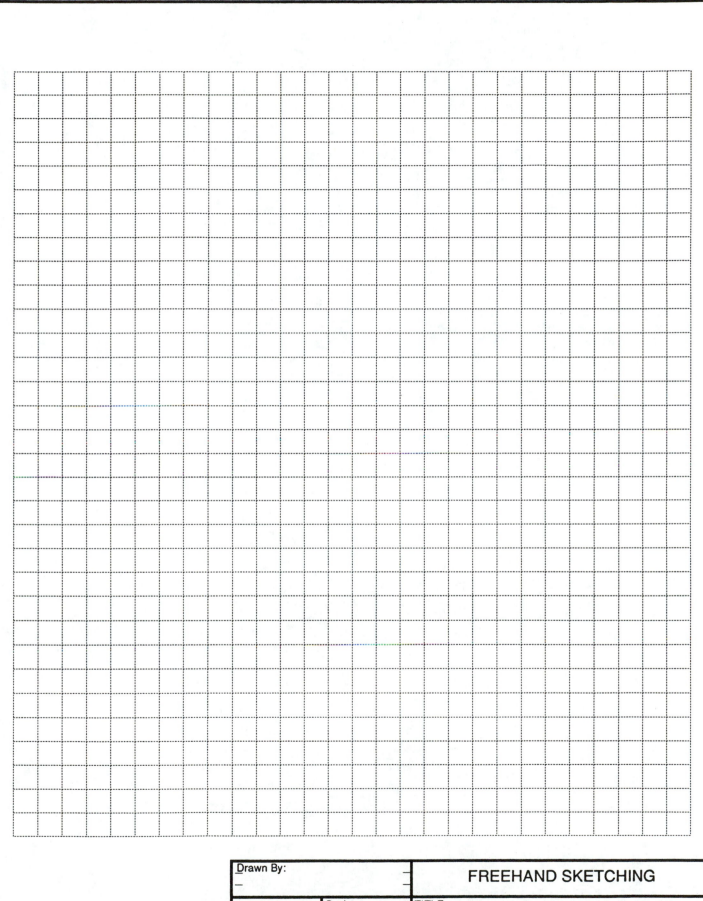

Drawn By:			FREEHAND SKETCHING	
	Scale	TITLE	ORTHOGRAPHIC GRID SHEET	
Date	Sheet of	Drawing Number	A	

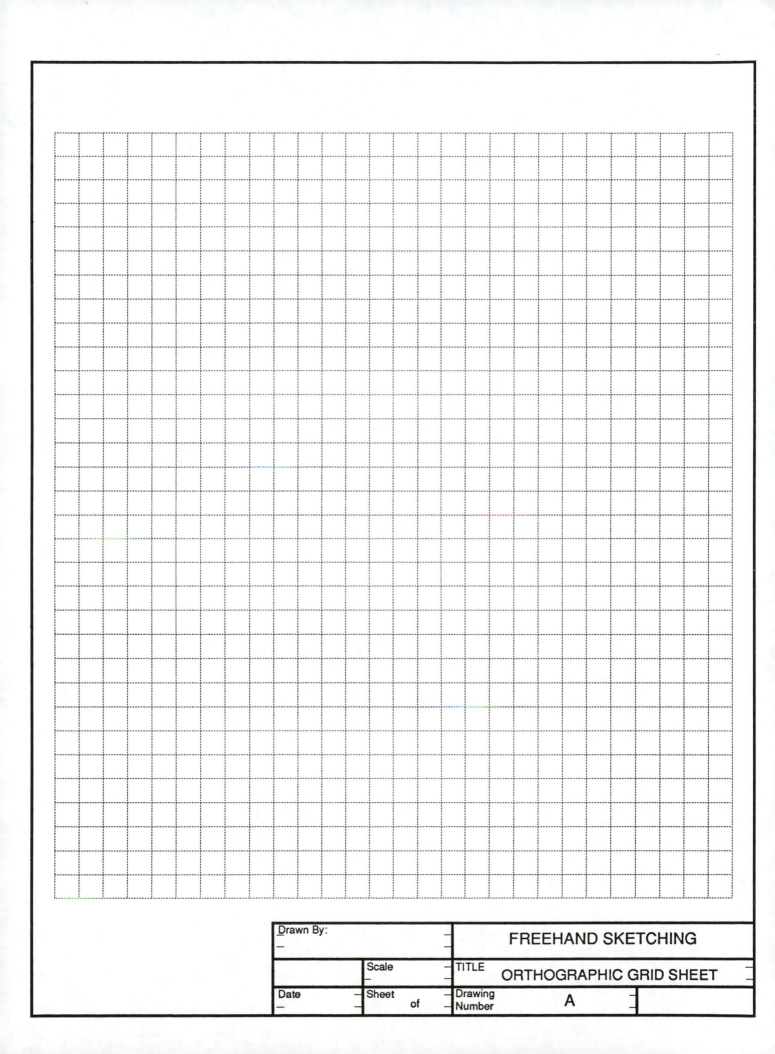

Drawn By:			FREEHAND SKETCHING	
	Scale		TITLE ORTHOGRAPHIC GRID SHEET	
Date	Sheet	of	Drawing Number	A

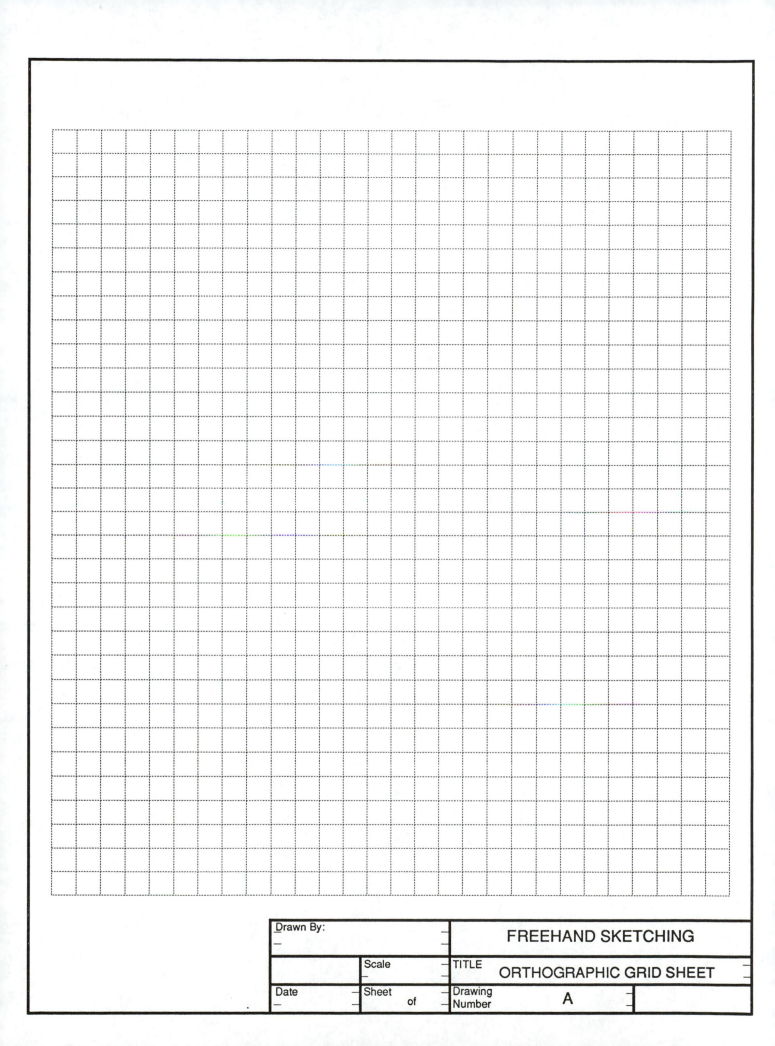

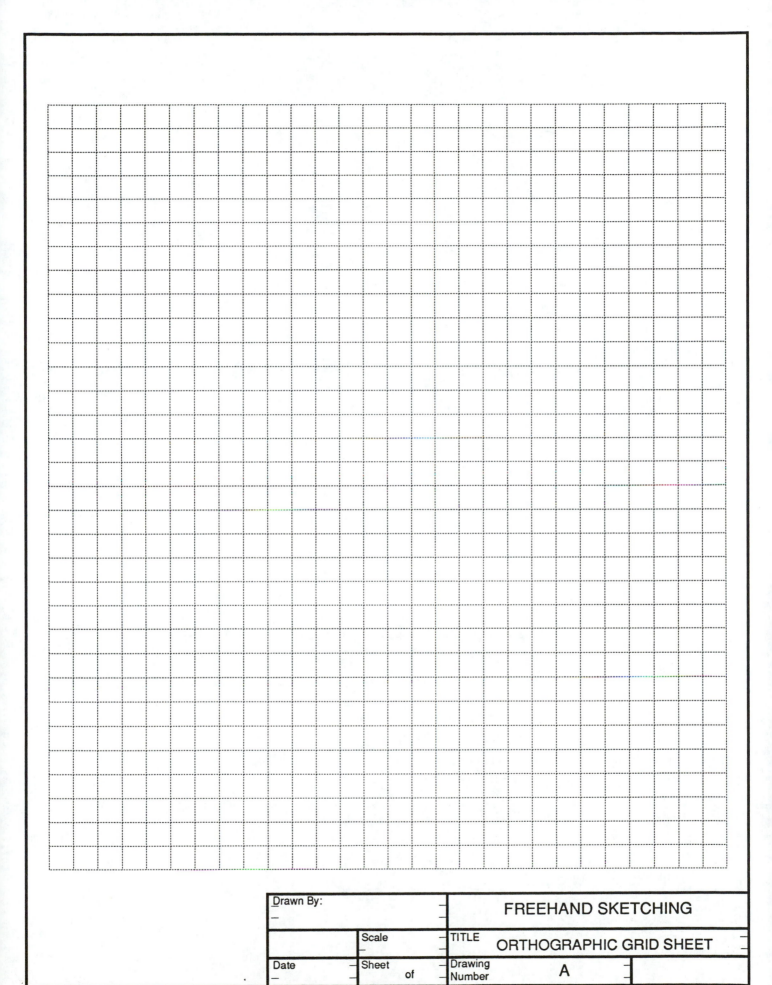

Drawn By:			FREEHAND SKETCHING	
	Scale	TITLE	ORTHOGRAPHIC GRID SHEET	
Date	Sheet of	Drawing Number	A	

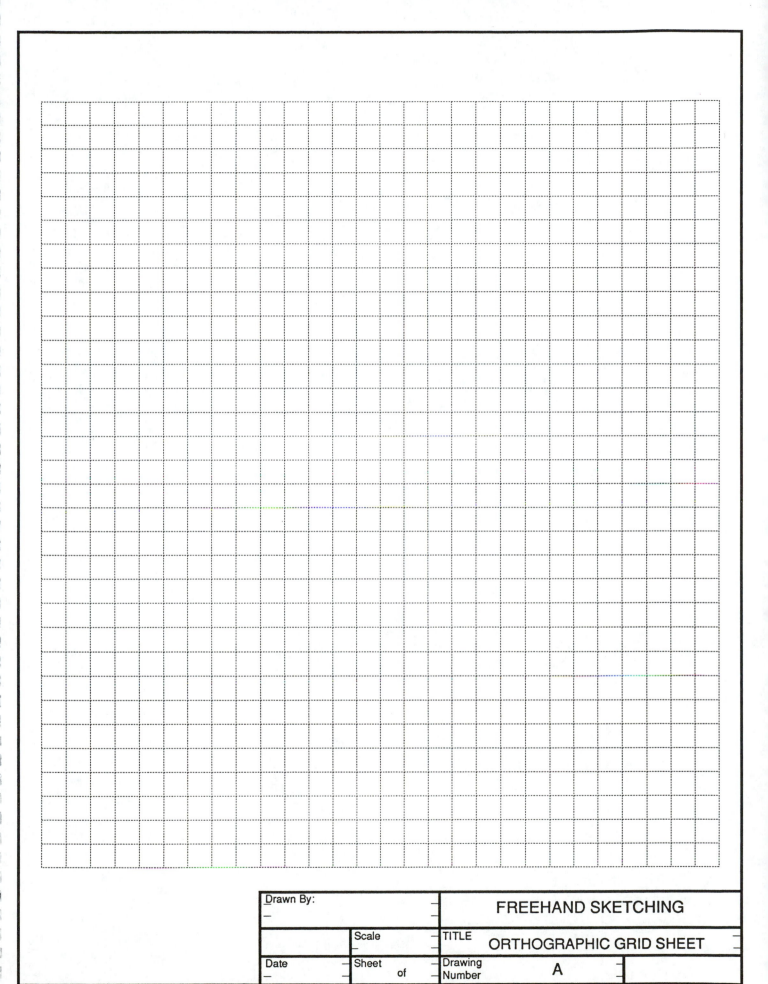

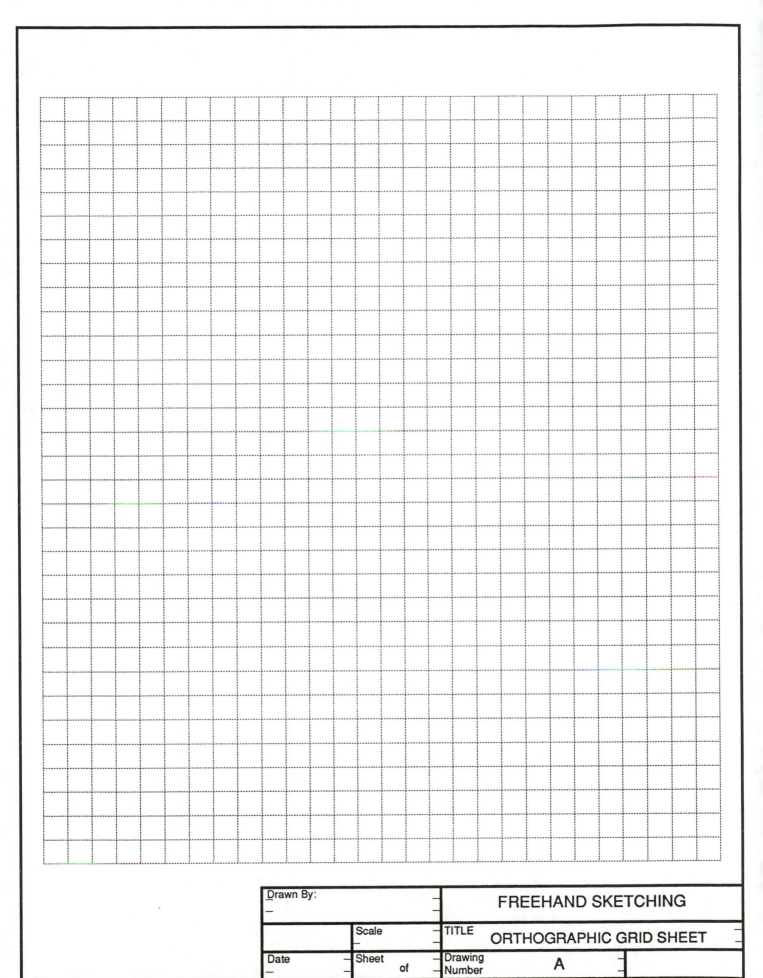

Drawn By:			FREEHAND SKETCHING	
	Scale		TITLE ORTHOGRAPHIC GRID SHEET	
Date	Sheet	of	Drawing Number	A

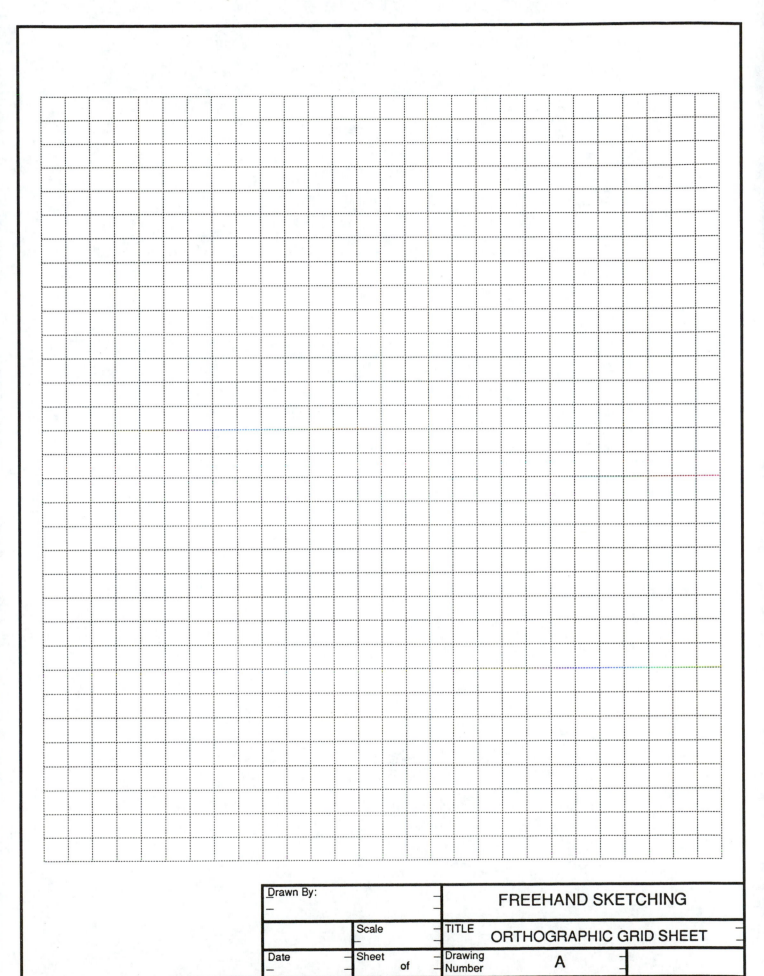

Drawn By:			FREEHAND SKETCHING	
	Scale		TITLE	ISOMETRIC GRID SHEET
Date	Sheet	of	Drawing Number	A

Drawn By:			FREEHAND SKETCHING	
	Scale		TITLE ISOMETRIC GRID SHEET	
Date	Sheet of		Drawing Number	A

Drawn By:			FREEHAND SKETCHING	
	Scale		TITLE ISOMETRIC GRID SHEET	
Date	Sheet	of	Drawing Number	A

Drawn By:			FREEHAND SKETCHING	
	Scale	TITLE	ISOMETRIC GRID SHEET	
Date	Sheet of	Drawing Number	A	

Drawn By:				FREEHAND SKETCHING	
	Scale		TITLE	ISOMETRIC GRID SHEET	
Date	Sheet	of	Drawing Number	A	

Drawn By:		FREEHAND SKETCHING	
	Scale	TITLE	ISOMETRIC GRID SHEET
Date	Sheet of	Drawing Number	A